# SIKHS

Nilanjan Mukhopadhyay embarked on a career in journalism in the early 1980s and is best known for his reportage and analysis of the rise and growth of Hindu organisations, their politics and agitations. He was among the first journalists to track the emergence of the Ram Janmabhoomi-Babri Masjid conflict from the late 1980s. He has followed, and written about, the political and electoral emergence of the BJP and its allies from that period.

He is the author of *The Demolition: India at the Crossroads* (1994), one of the first books on the Ayodhya discord and the rise of Hindutva. His biography of Narendra Modi, *Narendra Modi: The Man, the Times*, was published in early 2013, before Modi's campaign to become prime minister took off. It is widely considered the most credible and authoritative account of Modi's rise to power.

Mukhopadhyay is also the author of *The RSS: Icons of the Indian Right* (2019). His most recent book, *The Demolition and the Verdict: Ayodhya and the Project to Reconfigure India*, was published in 2021. He is a regular columnist in, and contributor to, several leading newspapers and web portals, and a well-known commentator and host on Indian television news and video channels. An unabashed college dropout, he lives in India's National Capital Region.

# SIKHS

## the untold agony of 1984

# Nilanjan Mukhopadhyay

WESTLAND
NON·FICTION

First published by Tranquebar Press, an imprint of Westland Ltd, in 2015

Published by Westland Non-Fiction, an imprint of Westland Books, a division of Nasadiya Technologies Private Limited, in 2023

No. 269/2B, First Floor, 'Irai Arul', Vimalraj Street, Nethaji Nagar, Allappakkam Main Road, Maduravoyal, Chennai 600095

Westland, the Westland logo, Westland Non-Fiction and the Westland Non-Fiction logo are the trademarks of Nasadiya Technologies Private Limited, or its affiliates.



ISBN: 9789395767538

10 9 8 7 6 5 4 3 2 1



Typeset by PrePSol Enterprises Pvt. Ltd
Printed at Saurabh Printers Pvt. Ltd

For Varsha

*Lighthouse on my stormy nights, anchor in choppy waters*

# Contents

# Author's Note

This book was born out of pain and I felt no joy after completing it. Just a sense of great relief.

A big dilemma from the outset was to use the accurate term to describe one of the most shameful episodes in post-Independent India -- was it an incident? Or, simply put, anti-Sikh riots? Or, perhaps it was a 'carnage'; however, the word pogrom seemed politically more correct, given the orchestrated nature of the violence.

Eventually, sticking to a single word for reference became a losing battle. After a while, I allowed the word to select itself, and chose not to be obdurate. Regardless of the word, this was an episode most vile, during which murders committed were most foul, and the political orchestration clearly macabre.

Every character you read about in this book is real and living her/his life in Delhi and elsewhere; some are well known, while several others are nondescript. But they are all linked by an experience which altered their lives indelibly.

I came to Delhi in 1979 when it was almost an overgrown village. The Sikhs were a respected lot and their language, Punjabi, a familiar tongue and almost a survival tool for people like me. When the city's demography altered dramatically (for reasons mentioned in the book), Sikhs were no longer perceived to be interchangeable with the Punjabiyat that was quintessentially Delhi at one time; over the years, fluency in Punjabi became irrelevant. Most importantly, in the increasing trend to rewrite or obliterate history, little or no memories of the 1984 riots remained.

For a nation such as ours, the excuse of selective or short memory is undoubtedly shameful. Almost twenty-nine years after the riots which shook the nation, the Delhi Sikh Gurudwara Management Committee or DSGMC in June 2013 finally decided to lay the foundation stone for a memorial in the Rakabganj Sahib

Complex for those who had lost their lives in the aftermath of Indira Gandhi's assassination.

Yet, this was anything but a collective atonement for the tragedy; the monument was yet another symptom of accusations and counter-accusations in a larger political game. The Committee, dominated by members of the Shiromani Akali Dal (SAD) and Bharatiya Janata Party or BJP decided that the five head priests or Panj Pyaras of the Sikh community would only be accompanied by leaders of the two parties for the foundation-laying ceremony, while the Congress and the Aam Aadmi Party (AAP) were kept out of the event. Gradually for the BJP-SAD combine, 1984 became a 'legitimate' reason for specious arguments at any given mention of the 2002 Gujarat riots.

It took another four years before the memorial, ironically called the Wall of Truth, was inaugurated in January 2017 and for once, political leaders stayed away  from the event because of two main reasons: first, there were elections in Punjab and second, large number of victims had already gathered to give the event ample strength. The Wall of Truth was testimony to the sacrifices made by scores of people – the sundry names inscribed on it included even those who had died protecting their Sikh neighbours and acquaintances.

Yet, it was no coincidence that work on the much-delayed memorial was speeded up after Sajjan Kumar, one of the main accused in the anti-Sikh riots, was acquitted by a lower court in Delhi in 2013. The collective outrage that followed after he was let off, galvanised the DSGMC into moving swiftly on the construction of the monument, lest it lost credibility amongst the community.

In December 2018, judges of the Delhi High Court sentenced Sajjan Kumar, by then seventy-three, to life imprisonment for the 'remainder of his natural life', and added amongst other things, that he had evaded arrest due to 'political patronage'. I spoke to Nirpreet Kaur, whose story is detailed in the book, and who was a principal litigant in the case and doggedly pursued it at a great personal cost, shortly after the conviction when it was certain that

Sajjan Kumar had no option but to turn himself in. His conviction, she said, had reinforced her faith in the Indian judicial system and convinced her that justice could not be denied indefinitely. She remained hopeful that other convictions shall follow even as Sajjan Kumar continued to petition the Supreme Court hoping to be released on parole.

When I asked Nirpreet if she was finally happy, she sounded melancholic and wasn't her usual blunt self: 'After 1984, there is nothing in my life except pain. His conviction came as a relief, but gives me no joy,' she added.

In time, if other convictions should follow, I wonder if it will succeed in alleviating the personal and collective pain of those who lost their lives in Independent India? This is one of the most  painful chapters in contemporary India which will keep resurfacing every now and then. I have noticed how many amongst the younger generation manifest both shock and horror at the gruesome narratives involving 1984. But like every other dark chapter in the history of a nation, these stories must live on because even in the darkest moment, it's a reminder that the strong and fortunate survive.  This book is a small contribution towards that...

# Characters, in No Order of Appearance

Harmeet Kaur: A middle class Delhi girl born several years after 1984

Swaranpreet Singh: A post-graduate medical student in Delhi, 1984; now based in London and more than a doctor at the time of writing

H S Phoolka: A lawyer in his Twenties in 1984; spearheaded the legal struggle for the survivors of 1984

Nirpreet Kaur: A teenager who lost her father in 1984; married a militant and jailed on terror charges; witness and crusader in cases against Congress leaders

Shanti Devi: Committed suicide after the pogrom; survived by two daughters

Jarnail Singh: Former journalist who chucked a shoe at ex-Home Minister, P Chidambaram; Member, Delhi Legislative Assembly since February 2015

Wing Commander (Late) Randhir Singh Chhatwal: Retired in 1984; active in relief and rehabilitation measures in 1984; also at the forefront of legal and political campaigns

Jasmeet Kaur: Born in 1984; now married into a lower-middle class family; resident of Ghaziabad (UP)

K J Singh: Ace sound engineer in Bollywood and Indian music industry; father of Hartej aka Teji

Surjit Kaur: Lost her husband and a son in 1984; resident of widow's colony, Garhi, South Delhi

Kulbir Singh: Human rights activist since 1984

Joginder Singh: A middle-aged ironsmith in 1984; resident of Trilokpuri, East Delhi

Jasmeet Singh: A ten year old in 1984; runs a mobile repair shop in an East Delhi market

Rahul Bedi: Senior journalist; among the first to write about the 1984 violence in Trilokpuri, East Delhi

Safina Uberoi: Daughter of academics—Patricia and J P S Uberoi; a schoolgirl in 1984; now an independent filmmaker

Brigadier Gurmeet Kanwal: A Captain in the Indian Army in 1984; now an accomplished strategic affairs commentator

Prabhsahay Kaur: Daughter of H S Phoolka; born a few months after October 1984; now a human rights lawyer

Gurpreet Kaur aka Behan Chaurasi: Born weeks after October 1984; became an *amritdhari* Sikh after marriage

Arvind Bedi: Worked in the security wing of Delhi Electric Supply Undertaking in 1984

Sewa Singh: Former assistant public relations officer, Sindri Fertiliser Plant, Dhanbad (Bihar); now an activist assisting survivors of the 1984 carnage

Paramjit Kaur: A child of 15 in 1984; now a medical doctor in Bokaro (Jharkhand)

Iqbal Singh: A thirty-year-old businessman in Gomoh (Jharkhand), in 1984

Vishy Kuruganti: A schoolboy in Bokaro in the early 1980s

Chandrima Ray: A schoolteacher in Bokaro (Jharkhand)

Jasbinder Grewal: A classmate of Vishy Kuruganti and Chandrima; now a resident of Chicago (USA)

Priti Haneja: Another batchmate of Vishy, Chandrima and Jasbinder;  now divides her time between Bengaluru and Pune

Surinder Pal Singh: Twenty something and unemployed in 1984; now Administrator, Bokaro Hospital

Joginder Singh Johal: Son of Darbara Singh, former chief minister of Punjab; hotelier and  liquor dealer in Dhanbad (Bihar)

A K Roy: Marxist and former  Member of Parliament from Dhanbad (Bihar)

Gurdip Singh: Migrated from Ranchi in 1984; now resident of Amritsar

Mandip Singh: A child in 1984; now a struggling businessman in Kanpur (UP)

Mokham Singh:  A successful businessman and community leader in Kanpur (UP)

Alok Mukhopadhyay: Country head, OXFAM in 1984; now Chief Executive, VHAI

Jaya Jaitley: One of the pioneers of the crafts movement in India; now a political and social activist

Aseem Srivastava: A college student in 1984; now an environmental economist and activist

Dinesh Mohan: Social activist and Professor Emeritus at the Indian Institute of Technology, Delhi

Mita Bose: Professor of English in Indraprastha College for Women, Delhi University

Lalita Ramdas: Social activist and wife of Admiral L Ramdas, former naval chief and Lokpal, Aam Aadmi Party

And several others...

# ONE

# Doomsday Delhi

**D**usk was settling over an autumnal Delhi. She gritted her teeth as molten wax from the candle she held aloft trickled down and solidified at the base of her nails. But she overcame the pain each time by looking at the tear-stricken faces of women standing in a semicircle of which she also became a part. Every now and then she also glanced at the group of children squatting on a metalled road holding candles in the air – unconcerned that every few minutes, a blob of wax gained enough momentum to flow down and settle at the base of their thumbs. It was the first day of November and people had gathered at Delhi's "Hyde Park"—the area around Jantar Mantar. It was protest as usual, just as it had been the previous year, the one before the previous, and the previous....

But that evening, it was Harmeet Kaur's first ever. She had come to join a group of both Sikhs and non-Sikhs drawn by an actor-friend's call who was playing multiple roles in a street play at the protest site. The friend had come all the way from Patiala – almost 250 kilometres away—as part of a small troupe of theatre activists from the Punjabi Rang Manch. In the course of a forty-five-minute action-packed performance, the actor alternated between enacting a mastermind of killer goons, a pleading survivor, and even a kerosene-spraying hooligan, whose macabre laughter pierced the wails of his fellow actors every time he lit a make-belief matchstick to cowering victims, who turned into imaginary balls of flame.

The 1991-born Harmeet Kaur was the elder of the two children born in quick succession, a decade after their parents' marriage. The younger brother lived and worked  in Mumbai as a trainee chef at the city's iconic Taj Mahal Palace Hotel – a career he eventually wanted to pursue. That evening, Harmeet had come straight from the government school where she worked as a trainee teacher while studying alongside to become a graduate. Later, much after the protest was over, Harmeet returned home and shared her experiences with her parents.

She switched on the television and located PTC, the Punjabi channel which she knew would carry a long story on the protest. Her dialogue with her parents drowned the voice-over  even as she identified the weeping widows—names which meant little to the uninitiated but held keys to countless tragedies... At some point while narrating the events, Harmeet's voice began to quiver, while her mother was more forthcoming and wept openly.  Her father remained the tough, stoic patriarch she had always known him to be.

Middle-class families in India seldom endorse public protests and particularly children's participation in them. But her father made no attempt to stop Harmeet. Her mother had in fact encouraged her to step out in an act of solidarity with the survivors of the 1984 carnage. The parents used the time-tested and simple logic of a "good cause" and heard in patience as their daughter neglected food on the plate and partially enacted the episodes of the evening—right from the street play to when the children arranged the candles in a neat 1984-like pattern.

In Harmeet's family, where involvement in politics was restricted to preparing campaign material and managing polling booths during elections to the Delhi Sikh Gurudwara Management Committee (DSGMC), for perhaps a cousin and his wife, open participation in a public protest begged investigation. What had led to the change or rather her interest in an issue which had political overtones? The stories she had heard from her parents about the aftermath of Indira Gandhi's assassination in 1984 or was it something else?

Harmeet went to a school in her neighbourhood which was managed by the DSGMC. Most of her classmates and teachers were  Sikhs but she had failed to fathom why there were many who were also *called* Sikhs but did not have long hair like her father or male-cousins. However, once or twice someone had told her, albeit casually, how men had cut their hair to save their lives during the  riots in 1984. A bit later, when the eleven-year-old Harmeet began taking private tuitions at a Sikh gent's house, she noticed the carpeted floor in the entire house. Curious queries directed at elders revealed that the house had been burnt down and as the inhabitants had never managed to get it repaired, the floor retained the scalded look. As a young woman in 2014, Harmeet believed that the family had consciously chosen to live with the pain of living in a burnt house. An ironical keepsake of merciless times!

The pre-teen Harmeet was an inquisitive child and joined other classmates to dig out more about 1984 from her parents and other friends. Soon, tales tumbled out and she had a little repertoire of gruesome stories—how several had been burnt to death; or escaped by hiding atop bus stops! For instance, the father of her classmate... Once when she narrated the incident on the dining table, her mother told her that they had luckily been on the *safe side* of the riotous mobs. Fortunate, but on a route where bravado had eluded them. Heartless though it may seem, the survivors of 1984 were bound by a common strand of victimhood. Sadly, escaping the rioters in the child's mind meant, exclusion from the victims' club!

Since Harmeet had had no direct links with the violence of 1984, she was drawn to public protests as a form of "atonement" for her parents' escape. Her parents also looked the other way because they had borne the burden of being *safe* for three decades whenever there were discussions within the community. Their daughter's act, they felt, would finally enable them to become part of the collective. Like any youngster her age, Harmeet dreamt of a future and sought guidance from this author for a career in television. But she was resolute that participating in protests was not a waste of time, which many of her peers endorsed.

Harmeet took recourse in an old cliché while assessing what she may have achieved by coming out that evening—drops can fill an ocean and if each individual stood up, there could be justice of some sort. While returning from the protest site, Harmeet resolved that this would not be a one-off participation and pledged her lifelong support for those whose lives had reversed in a matter of hours three decades ago.

The story of Harmeet's decision to join the protest and most importantly, her evolution in understanding one of the darkest subplots in contemporary Indian history, is not only unique to her but is simultaneously representative of her generation. She is both a solitary "Harmeet" and thousands of "Harmeet-like" youth. No one had fed them with tutorials in revenge—or else they wouldn't have been protesting peacefully. Their perception was built on collective memories, one nugget arranged after the other—a pattern in which truth may have become secondary. But they are impelled in their search by the belief that not enough was done. Her words—simple though—reverberated for long: 'I saw that woman crying... and kept thinking, why did she face so much pain; why does she still have to *fight* for justice?'

## 31 October 1984

Shortly after ten in the morning, an aspiring journalist and researcher in his early Twenties sat across a table in Alok Mukhopadhyay's office of the international donor agency, OXFAM.

Alok heard in rapt attention to the young man who was attacked some days ago in a central Indian industrial township along with a trade union leader by a group of hired henchmen.

The narrative was broken by a shrill ring of the telephone. Alok was silent for a long time before interjecting, 'How serious is she?' The conversation continued in murmurs and when it was over, Alok got up to indicate that he had to leave immediately.

'Mrs Gandhi has been shot. She's been rushed to the All India Institute of Medical Sciences (AIIMS). Come, let's go,' said Alok to the young man.

The road outside the hospital was teeming with people and like Alok and the other man, everyone had heard, but were reluctant to confirm the news. The police cordoning off the main gate of the hospital campus and barring entry without an identity card or a genuine and plausible reason, didn't seem convincing. Across the road, kiosks encroaching upon the pavement outside Safdarjung Hospital were doing business but the usual briskness was missing.

Alok and the young man stood gawking at the assembling crowds. Soon they were joined by the one who had presumably made the phone call. Despite the apparent hecticity, there was little to do, except wait. By noon, the BBC World Service had headlined its 12:30 bulletin by announcing that Indira Gandhi was critical, only to break into the broadcast a few minutes later to confirm that she was dead.

Some more people joined Alok and the other man. The conversation amongst them was desultory—for every word spoken, there were several that were not. At some point, someone in the crowd stirred and a few Sikhs were abused and jostled. By early evening, when the muted aggression on the streets was beginning to display signs of escalating, Alok suggested to the young man to head home.

The young journalist did not board the bus that would take him to the  room he shared with another journalist in a south Delhi colony. Instead he headed for another friend's house, where over the next few days he went through life-altering experiences. Once he overcame the struggle to get past the footboard in the jam-packed DTC bus on route no. 666, he unspooled the reels—truth be told, he had always been a critic of Indira Gandhi from his university days where anti-establishment rhetoric was fashionable—but to accept that she had been *assassinated;* someone who had seemed invincible, was beyond belief. In retrospect, he hardly understood the dynamics of the Punjab problem, and had gone along with his peers about how Mrs Gandhi had encouraged a section of militants to counter the Akali Dal in the state. Yet, this was not the kind of closure he would have wanted for the Indian Prime Minister. But as the evening progressed, his analyses appeared absurd and an overwhelming sense of uncertainty took over about the impending night....

Almost three decades later, he decided to write about this episode in India's contemporary history. The fruit of that labour is now in the hands of the reader.

Around the time I boarded the bus from AIIMS, Swaranpreet Singh was also running through details of the multiple sequences in his mind. On that morning of October 1984, we were barely a few yards away from each other, yet for the next thirty years we remained oblivious of the surreality despite shared memories and concerns.

That afternoon Swaranpreet was in—or so he thought then—the safe confines of his home in a middle class west Delhi colony and recollected the moment when he had parked his scooter in Safdarjung Hospital where he was interning to become a surgeon. The morning was etched frame by frame in his mind and so were the events that had forced him to give up surgery and take up psychiatry to specialise in post-trauma recovery.

Swaranpreet would have laughed if someone had prophesied that in less than two decades, he would cease to be an Indian citizen and have a Greek wife! Part of a small clan of Sikhs from Kashmir—originally Kashmiri Brahmins—Swaranpreet's father performed service in Sikh temples and despite starting life as an unlettered person, later went on to become a historian. He was obviously a man of modest means, but the family—including another son and a daughter—got by and lived comfortably.

Swaranpreet was a conscientious student in school, and graduated from the Government Medical College, Jammu in the summer of 1984. On 31 October, anticipating a fresh posting, the young doctor arrived in his grey-colour Chetak scooter which he parked in the usual place and went to the ward at the appointed time. Like others in the medical profession, Swaranpreet was used to nurses and other hospital staff being obsequious and was taken aback when the clerk who routinely informed him about his assignments, took off on seeing him.

'You bastards killed her!'

Swaranpreet realised instantly that the situation warranted action. The young doctor asked around: some said that there were rumours that Indira Gandhi had been gunned down by her Sikh bodyguards, while others were guarded in their replies. Swaranpreet ventured outside with a colleague and the two dressed in doctors' overalls, crossed the road and stayed inside the AIIMS campus for close to three hours. At some point, several dignitaries were seen inside AIIMS and many more after BBC's announcement of Indira Gandhi's death. By the time Swaranpreet's colleague advised him to go home, the road outside AIIMS was completely choked and even as he struggled to get out of the gate, there were mixed responses— someone swore at him, others were crying out of shock and some were genuinely grieving for the woman who lay dead inside the hospital. Suddenly, someone hit Swaranpreet on the back of his head. He reacted typically, as a Sikh would do in such a situation and held on to his turban. Years later, he would take it off permanently for completely different reasons and instead of feeling persecuted for being forced into a decision, he would feel relieved that he was finally able to make the choice. But on that afternoon, rapid blows rained on his head. Although he managed to escape without any serious injuries, it left him badly shaken.

Out on the street, he hailed an auto-rickshaw and  the non-Sikh driver agreed to take him home. On the way, Swaranpreet calmed himself down, stopped the auto-rickshaw midway and retied his turban. When he entered his house after more than an hour, he was convinced what he had witnessed on Delhi's streets was general outrage and nowhere near organised violence. He was forced to change his mind over the next couple of days, as he did in the following months and years....

Around the time Swaranpreet Singh crossed Aurobindo Marg and went into AIIMS, in another part of Delhi, Jaya Jaitley was on her way to the American Embassy along with George Fernandes, then a leader of the Janata Party and later India's Defence Minister. The duo had collected their visas for an international conference on "Democratic Socialism" and were returning when they noticed a comical road sign blocking the entry to Safdarjung Road, "Menat Work!" Jaya ignored the linguistic faux pas of the unknown NDMC supervisor with a smile, little realising that the intended phrase, "Men At Work" would acquire a deeper meaning in the hours that followed.

By late afternoon, Sujan Singh Park—a plush enclave of tony apartments on the edge of Lutyens' Delhi—was buzzing with "the news". Jaya and her ex-husband, Ashok Jailtey decided to head for AIIMS and had barely reached a short distance when they saw a mob thrashing several Sikhs in Jor Bagh. A small posse of policemen was engrossed in watching the spectacle. When the Jaitleys drew their attention to the "action" across the road, they were told to mind their own business. Why were they so agitated? After all they weren't Sikhs! This overt display of police inaction eventually became a recurring feature of the law enforcing agencies  in the capital.

The Jaitleys meanwhile headed further down the road. A car was aflame close to the point where the narrower  Lodhi Road merged with the arterial Aurobindo Marg, barely two kilometres away from AIIMS. A crowd had gathered around the burning vehicle and there was talk about  how Sikhs were being thrown off the Safdarjung Road flyover after being plucked out of their vehicles. The Jaitleys also noticed two or three Sikhs who had parked their two-wheelers near a footpath, and appeared terrified and unsure of what to do next. Jaya and Ashok stopped in front of them, and took them home by a safer route. Later in the afternoon, they decided to drop the men back to their homes but by then restive crowds were stopping every car on the street to look for Sikhs. It was well past midnight when the Jaitleys finally took them to the Tughlaq Road Police Station and asked the policemen on duty to escort them back. Their scooters remained parked outside the Jaitleys' apartment till January 1985. Jaya Jaitley never got to know the names of the three men. This story, in any case, did not need that detail....

Far away from the crowd of anxious Delhiites on the stretch of Aurobindo Marg outside AIIMS, there was an exciting draw at Indraprastha (IP) College, one of Delhi University's celebrated women's colleges. Squadron Leader Rakesh Sharma, the first Indian to go into space, and his Air Force colleague, Ravish K Malhotra were in the college as special invitees. A felicitation ceremony was underway and after addressing the students, a light-hearted Q&A session followed, the kind where Sharma was almost invariably asked about his response to Indira Gandhi when he had quipped, *Saare jahaan se achcha* in reply to his premier's query on how India looked from his space station.

The bantering continued on stage when a couple of Air Force officers strode up to confer with Sharma and Malhotra and before anyone could comprehend the situation, the duo got up and told the hosts that they had to leave owing to a pressing matter. The students and staff were still deliberating on their next move when a teacher received a call from her husband, who was a senior neurosurgeon in AIIMS. In a few moments, everyone knew in the campus. But not what was to follow....

❈ ❈ ❈ ❈

About the time when Wing Commander Rakesh Sharma and his colleague left IP College, Anil Nauriya was waiting for his case to come up before Justice P N Bhagwati in the Supreme Court. The Registrar approached the Judge and whispered something into his ear. Another member of the Supreme Court Bench who was hearing the matter along with Justice Bhagwati, also joined in the conversation. The three confabulated for an inordinately long period after which the judges got up and told the lawyers that they would be back shortly.

The judges returned and resumed the hearing but did not rise for the day as they were still awaiting an official confirmation of the prime minister's murder. Later, Nauriya decided to visit the *Hindustan Times* office on Kasturba Gandhi Marg, one of the radial exits from Connaught Place, where he once worked. By then another newspaper, *The Statesman* had put out a "spot-news" outside its office: Indira Gandhi Shot.

"Mrs Gandhi assassinated", said the *Indian Express* and even the normally circumspect *Hindustan Times* announced: "Indira Gandhi is dead", indicating that even in the absence of an official announcement, there was no doubt that the Indian Prime Minister was dead.

In newspaper offices, judgements were being formed. One of Nauriya's ex-colleagues sounded harsh. I'm not sorry, she said. Nauriya replied with a question: Who will it help? Even before the blood had begun coagulating in the body that was lying in an emergency facility at AIIMS, opinions had begun flying back and forth. Some articulated their thoughts, while others took recourse to action....

❈ ❈ ❈ ❈

The judges of Delhi High Court didn't have the authority their seniors wielded in the apex court. As a result, they continued working without a break even after the rumours spread. Close to noon, word spread that Indira Gandhi had been shot by two men with the same surnames: Singh. H S Phoolka*, a young Sikh lawyer who had recently shifted to the Indian capital from Chandigarh was a worried man. A colleague assuaged his fears that Singh did not necessarily mean Sikhs and that surnames were not religion-specific!

Soon there was confirmation that the assassins were indeed Sikhs and Phoolka was reminded of how the police would hunt for them in rickety buses... (in recent months, after a spate of terrorist attacks on Hindus, even ordinary Sikhs had come under the scanner). He immediately got on to his scooter and headed for west Delhi where his pregnant wife worked as a food technologist.

When he reached his wife's office at 3:00 pm, it seemed like any other working day. His wife told him that she couldn't leave before 5:00, which was the scheduled close of work. He returned at the appointed hour and they made their way to his office in Connaught Place before heading for home. They were surprised that despite the news of the assassination, everything seemed so *normal* in Delhi.

❋ ❋ ❋ ❋

The students of Delhi School of Economics were quick to react once the rumours spread. During a break, Aseem Srivastava—who later became an accomplished environmental economist—and a few of his friends found someone who had a radio and tuned in to the BBC news bulletin. The news appeared incredulous—'a bit like the meltdown of the Everest,' recalled Aseem. Although the All India Radio (AIR) hadn't made an official  announcement, it was ominously playing a sarangi recital, reserved strictly for national tragedies. This confirmed the worst and students made their way to the bus stand in front of Hindu College.

---

* He later became a crusader for the victims of the anti-Sikh pogrom and eventually joined politics, but lost the 2014 Lok Sabha elections as a candidate of the Aam Aadmi Party or AAP.

On his way home, Aseem felt something unusual on the streets of Delhi. He noticed that although  people looked shaken and mournful, there were no signs of violent behaviour—it was as if they had resolved to grieve quietly for the departed leader. Since everything seemed peaceful, Aseem decided to drop by at a friend's house in a colony of senior government employees. But by the time he headed home around 9:00 pm, the streets of Delhi had transformed. There were mobs hunting for Sikhs inside buses. Suddenly, 1947 seemed real and with it the Partition. It wasn't a distant year in the calendar any more, the one about which he had heard but never bothered.

Years later, whenever he ran past the memories of that fateful day, Aseem felt it was the real beginning of the country's descent into barbarism. 31 October 1984 became the turning point in his life, and steered him away from what his father had desired. It was at this juncture when Aseem embarked on a definite path and fostered relationships which sustained  for the rest of his life.

Safina Uberoi's  life changed despite her young age and because of which she was also spared the scenes  of violence that followed Indira Gandhi's assassination. She was on the verge of finishing high school and grappling with her identity: who am I in relation to my family, relatives and friends? This sorting out of identity was not the usual existentialist phase common at her age, but relevant because of her interracial and multicultural heritage: her father was a goatee-sporting, short-haired academic with Sikh roots, while her mother was Australian—also an academic who chose to make India her home when the man she loved decided to move back and raise his family in India.

Safina was troubled by these questions and carried them to school on the morning of 31 October 1984. Till a few months ago, she was a half-white child, but now she felt like a *Sikh* child. During this process of "conversion", she also turned to religion, from being completely oblivious to it till recently.

Aadmi Party which he lost. He returned to the electoral arena in the 2015 Delhi assembly polls, this time successfully. But neither the shoe-chucking incident, nor his political indoctrination hinged on his Sikh identity....

Dr Dinesh Mohan may be best known as a bio-medical engineer, retired IIT professor, an urban transport expert, but he insists on adding yet another identity to the long list and that is of a voyeur! On 31 October 1984 after news about Indira's Gandhi's murder, he picked up his AIIMS faculty card which he had been issued because the two institutes ran a collaborative research programme, and remembered to carry his small Leica camera along. At twelve noon, just as Dr Mohan was entering AIIMS, he witnessed scuffles. A few Sikhs were being jostled even though there was no official confirmation of Sikhs' involvement in the murder of Mrs Gandhi. At one place he saw a Sikh's turban being lit on fire. The scientist promptly took a picture of this symbolic obliteration of Sikh identity – an act which was repeated several times in the next few days. A year later, he filed an affidavit in the Misra Commission— the first of the many panels of enquiry set up over the next two decades. Dr Mohan's pictures became part of the proceedings, particularly of a policeman averting his gaze when Sikhs were being chased and abused on the streets of the nation's capital.

In October 1984, Jasmeet Kaur was barely forty-five days old when her mother had taken the "still unnamed one" for the customary post-natal visit to her parents' home in Gurgaon, Haryana. It is therefore obvious that Jasmeet Kaur only had second-hand account of the violence in the aftermath of Mrs Gandhi's assassination, in the form of oral narratives from members of her family. But ironically, Jasmeet grew up associating the riots with her ill-timed birth—as the harbinger of misfortune in the home of her maternal grandfather.

Within hours of their arrival in faraway Gurgaon, violence had broken out in the locality and over the next few days, Jasmeet's mother along with her new-born baby took refuge in neighbourhood homes. The young mother helplessly watched her home being burnt, looted and vandalised and ever since, Jasmeet was never allowed to forget how grown-ups in the family would often clamp her tiny mouth—even risking asphyxiation— to stop her from crying, lest the marauding mobs hunted down the family. Three decades and several other events later, Jasmeet continues to feel hunted and manifests extreme nervousness, fear of strangers, and a reluctance to open up to new people. Despite a Bachelors in Education and Masters in English, she finds it difficult to even drive down to a nearby market to shop for essential goods.

When I asked her if there is a child inside her who refuses to grow up and is chased by phantom figures, Jasmeet smiled uncomfortably....

❅ ❅ ❅ ❅

Unlike Jasmeet who retreated into a shell because of infantile trauma, Nirpreet Kaur sought retribution and made it her lifelong mission. But before she became a crusader in the battle for justice for survivors of the 1984 violence, Nirpreet was like any other teenager—a good student and the darling daughter of her father who was a successful transporter and dealer in the sale and supply of building material in Palam Colony. 31 October 1984 began like any other day for the young girl and even when news of Indira Gandhi's death was beginning to seep through the layers of Delhi, Nirpreet had no premonition of the impending doom.

The gurudwara or Sikh temple in the locality that was to be torched within the next few hours, was still intact. Her father Nirmal Singh, who would be set ablaze and left to die by a mob led by political leaders barely twenty-four hours later, was negotiating a business deal with a man who eventually played a vital role in his killing....

It was a day on which Wing Commander Randhir Singh Chhatwal had completed one month of post-retirement life after three decades of service in the Indian Air Force. He had a few pension-related matters to resolve at the Air Headquarters in Lutyens Delhi and drove down on his old scooter. After news of the PM's killing, officials at the Air Headquarters called it a day and Chhatwal left for home well before 1:00 pm.

He drove through the wide avenues of Delhi's bungalow zone before reaching the flyover that overlooked the famed Oberoi Hotel and stopped as his scooter sputtered to a halt indicating a clog in the spark plug. Chhatwal sat on his haunches, got down to the task and  wondered if anyone else on the streets had heard of the shootout at 1, Safdarjang Road.

Like several other Sikhs, Chhatwal had also been critical of Indira Gandhi's handling of Punjab and Operation Blue Star but had desisted from voicing it in public—as a member of India's defence forces, he showed caution. After fixing his scooter, Wing Commander Chhatwal stood on the flyover and secured a moment with his inner self. He was definitely not elated at the death of Indira Gandhi. Strangely, his  thoughts went to the festival of Guru Purab or the birth anniversary of Guru Nanak the next day and the ritual of Prabhat Pheri, with musicians walking the streets at the crack of dawn singing devotional songs. Chhatwal was among its organisers and concluded that given the circumstances, the Prabhat Pheri should be a quiet affair lest it's mistaken for a celebratory march.

Chhatwal made arrangements to exclude the drummers the next morning and returned home. Lunch with his wife was a quiet affair—the two ate, oblivious to the fact that one of them would be deeply involved in seeking redressal. Chhatwal's post-retirement life was in absolute contrast to his service years and he remained engaged in it till 16 November 2013, the day he passed on from life....

❖ ❖ ❖ ❖

Twenty-three-year-old Kanwarjit Singh Sawhney aka K J Singh, who the world would later come to recognise as India's foremost sound engineer, was on a song that morning. Born into affluence in a family that  supplied meat products to army messes, K J typified the Eighties generation which experimented with life and veered off the beaten tracks. Despite occasional suggestions by his father to get involved in the family's other business of running petrol and diesel stations in Agra, K J Singh enrolled for a Masters programme at Delhi University as the two-year hiatus gave him time to decide his future.

One day, egged on by his desire to venture into the unknown, K J Singh met the well-known newscaster, Komal G B Singh in Doordarshan, who also ran a recording studio. As luck would have it, she offered him a job to man the recording machines in her studio and K J Singh embarked on a career as sound engineer, distanced himself from the family business and most importantly, decided to pursue the love of his life, Poonam.

On the evening of 31 October 1984, the young couple headed towards Mandi House, the cultural hub of the capital known for  the building that gave the roundabout and its surroundings its name. The two had planned to catch a play at the Shri Ram Centre besides grabbing a bite of crispy *pakoras*. Although a "Play Cancelled" sign was visible at the entrance of the theatre, they whiled away time before K J Singh eventually reached home close to 9:00 pm. Many years later, K J Singh would shudder to think of the violence that had broken out within minutes of his driving past several spots that eventually became theatres of violence against his community....

❖ ❖ ❖ ❖

Surjit Kaur was a long way from home the day Indira Gandhi was shot. A resident of Nand Nagri in east Delhi, she had ventured out with her three sisters-in-law to meet a relative in Ashok Vihar in the northern part of the Indian capital. The bus ride had been long as usual and while doing the proverbial last mile by foot, the four women caught local residents whispering conspiratorially. Curious enquiries evinced nothing except doors slammed shut on their faces and a curt, 'Sorry, we do not know,' response. At their relatives' home, they got to know the reason and after a quick meal, decided to leave for Nand Nagri.

It was evening by the time the four managed to trudge back home. By then, Surjit's two sons—Kamaljit Singh and Tarvinder Singh, aged sixteen and thirteen respectively—had returned from school and were playing with friends in the locality. Shortly thereafter, her husband Joginder Singh who ran a modest garment export manufacturing unit in a government shed close by, returned home. It was a usual evening that was drawing to a close.

Surjit Kaur enquired of her husband if he had a peaceful day at work and was relieved after Joginder assured her how he had lunch with his regular non-Sikh friends, also owners of small manufacturing and tailoring units. He then looked at his wife's face and added that although he had heard the news by lunch hour, no one had said anything objectionable to him and this despite the fact that the shooters were Sikhs. As dusk fell over Delhi, Surjit and her husband shared a quiet moment over a cup of tea… their last twilight together.

❖ ❖ ❖ ❖

Around the time when Joginder Singh and his friends were gathering for lunch in his factory, life was changing irreversibly for the one time-pilot-turned-reluctant politician, Rajiv Gandhi. At 12:30 pm, while waiting at Calcutta (now Kolkata) airport for a flight to Delhi, he had tuned into BBC World Service. After a few minutes he had confirmation of what he had feared a couple of hours earlier when a police patrol had advised him to jettison his plans of addressing a campaign rally in the Hooghly Delta region in West Bengal.

Rajiv proceeded to share the information with Uma Shankar Dikshit, the then Governor of West Bengal and also a close loyalist of Indira Gandhi. Typical of the man who was known to be fiercely private, Rajiv sat one seat away from Dikshit. The two men remained quiet without intruding into each other's grief. Several minutes later, Rajiv Gandhi gathered his nerves and joined the pilots in the cockpit, like he had always done on previous occasions. In less than two hours, his friend and superstar, Amitabh Bachchan received him in Delhi  and after a quick word about the safety of his wife and children, Rajiv headed for AIIMS. There was no escaping his destiny.

Just when Rajiv Gandhi was gathering his wits at the Calcutta airport, Kulbir Singh was meeting his friend, Meghnad Bhattacharjee at People's Publishing House in Connaught Place. The shop housing the publishing unit of the Communist Party of India (located on the radial road exiting from the Outer Circle and merging into Panchkuian Road) was a popular hub and meeting ground for both young and old radicals in the city. The young men were headed towards New Delhi railway station to catch a train to Daltonganj in what was still Bihar. Although the train station was abuzz with news of the shooting incident, neither considered changing the plan, even though Kulbir *wore* what was later construed to be  the wrong flag on his head. An ebullient Sikh, he was a member of the People's Union for Democratic Rights (PUDR) and Meghnad was an upcoming filmmaker.

The young men in their Twenties boarded the train for a journey through hell. A voyage that jeopardised Kuldip Singh's life and scarred Meghnad permanently....

It was as if a select group of journalists and officials midair between Sana'a and New Delhi were privy to Rajiv Gandhi's karma and his place in history. A special flight was bringing back the then Indian President, Giani Zail Singh and his official entourage, in the wake of Indira Gandhi's assassination. On board with the President were officials of the President's Secretariat and several senior journalists including Inderjit of Indian News and Features Agency who later went on to become a Member of Parliament from Darjeeling; M K Dhar of the *Hindustan Times*; Satinder Singh from *The Tribune*; M K Joshi from *The Hindu* and the young and relatively junior, Prabhu Chawla (now Editorial Director of *The New Indian Express*)—probably the only one in that press party to have never met Indira Gandhi. He was however close to the President who confided a matter of national importance to him: Rajiv Gandhi was to be India's next prime minister.

From the airport, Zail Singh headed straight for the All India Institute of Medical Sciences. As his cavalcade drove through Delhi's streets around 5:00 pm on 31 October, it was accosted by a group of boisterous youngsters in Rama Krishna Puram, once a colony for mid- and lower-level government employees. Travelling inside the fourth car of the fleet was Sardar Tarlochan Singh, the then media advisor to the President and who later became the chairperson of National Minorities Commission and also an independent member of the Rajya Sabha. Singh's car was first blocked by the mob and then pelted with stones; someone even lit a tyre and came perilously close to stuffing it inside his car. In the melee, the rear windshield of the car broke into smithereens but the driver of the car demonstrated great presence of mind and dropped out of the presidential cavalcade and took a detour to Rashtrapati Bhawan. The aggression had assumed dangerous proportions by the time the President reached the entrance of the AIIMS campus. A huge unruly mob thronged the locked gate of the hospital and even after identifying the person in the big limousine, they made no attempts to give way.

After his visit to the hospital where he was officially informed of Indira Gandhi's death, Giani Zail Singh left immediately to ready himself for an important duty: to appoint Rajiv Gandhi Prime Minister. The usually resplendent Rashtrapati Bhawan wore a sombre look as necessitated by a great tragedy. A visibly shaken Tarlochan Singh went through the motions as did the President. The anger on the streets of Delhi was perhaps forgotten temporarily but worse was to follow.

The last time the country and especially Delhi had mourned collectively was in January 1948 when the "Father of the Nation" or Bapu was felled by a mad man's bullets. Nearly four decades later, the nation and its capital was horrified yet again by Indira Gandhi's murder, undoubtedly a brutal attack on a national leader of great stature. When unconfirmed reports began making the rounds on the morning of 31 October, Delhi was in a state of virtual paralyses as people groped around for an appropriate response to a great tragedy. The varied reactions to the assassination—some of which have been highlighted in this chapter—were therefore marked by the insignia of simultaneity of time. Unlike a natural catastrophe that binds victims to a  common cause, responses to a political calamity like Indira Gandhi's assassination were distinctly different. While some viewed it as devastating, leaving a nation orphaned; others viewed it through the political prism concluding that it was a natural fallout in which adversaries are often annihilated. A miniscule section rationalised the assassination but were careful to keep it private unless forced to share it with those endorsing their views. Sadly, although this section included large numbers of non-Sikhs, in public perception only Sikhs were seen to have held this opinion.

In 1984, Delhi was neither the fully-developed hydra-headed urban monstrosity that it eventually became in the 1990s, nor the pre-Seventies' idyllic semi-urban and sparsely populated tract of endless pastures of villages. In the second decade of the twentieth century, the change in Delhi's character was necessitated after the British shifted their capital from Calcutta and made Delhi the Imperial seat of power.

By 1941, Delhi was considered a large city by any standards, particularly after the official census figure pegged its population at approximately nine lakhs of which almost seven were urban dwellers and not residents of villages trapped within Delhi's growing urban expanse. However, due to the unprecedented migration during Partition, Delhi's demographic character altered overnight and it grew at an incredible rate of almost ninety per cent in the decade between 1941-51 and in comparison to several other cities in north India, it housed the maximum number of refugees after Partition. A city that was once defined as Indo-Islamic and hence both politically and "poetically" pluralistic, Delhi was transformed into a battlefield in 1947-48. Several images of the carnage in parts of the city after Indira Gandhi's assassination in 1984—of rotting bodies and filthy refugee camps —evoked a certain sense of déjà vu. W H Morris Jones in his essay, "Changing Delhi Through Changing Eyes" expressed shock after a visit to the Walled City or Shahjahanabad that 'the lanes were eerily deserted but not completely so; corpses lay uncollected, animals roamed...' This was also reminiscent of Delhi in November 1984.

An estimated 3.3 lakh Muslims left Delhi during Partition and were replaced by almost double the numbers comprising both Hindus and Sikhs. As a result, Delhi's character became prominently Punjabi and Punjabiyat became interchangeable with what was once Indo-Islamic. The number of Sikhs in the city went up significantly and in the first census undertaken after Independence in 1951, Delhi registered a Sikh population of more than 1.37 lakhs, a significant representation of 7.85 per cent, whereas previously they accounted for just a shade more than a per cent.

Thereafter, Delhi's population grew  dramatically in the decades after Independence as migration to urban centres began with great vigour and the capital finally metamorphosed into a mega metropolis—from 17.44 lakhs in 1951 to 62.2 lakhs in 1981, registering a decadal growth rate of more than fifty per cent, the highest being in the period between 1971-81, at 53 per cent. The Sikhs in Delhi also maintained a growth rate of 48.74 per cent in the initial period of 1951-61 and went up to 2.04 lakhs. But with no mass scale influx of Sikhs into Delhi in the post-Partition period, the percentage of Sikhs dipped marginally to 7.67 in 1961. The same trend continued till 1981 when 3.93 lakh Sikhs in the city accounted for 6.33 per cent of the population. But in the aftermath of the pogrom, the city witnessed large-scale migration of Sikhs and their numbers declined to 4.84 and 4.01 per cent in 1991 and 2001 respectively.

In the three decades after the events of 1984, Delhi's demographic character altered yet again. It was culturally no longer a "Punjabi" city, and was instead taken over by migrants from Uttar Pradesh and Bihar, who spoke a version of Hindi peppered with regional flavours from  their respective regions. In was also during this period when Delhi ceased to be a Union Territory and its status was constitutionally upgraded to that of a state, albeit with limited powers when compared to other "full-fledged states".

In October 1984, the Union Territory of Delhi was administered by the President through an Administrator, initially designated as Chief Commissioner but in later years "re-designated" as Lieutenant Governor. During the Sikh riots, P G Gavai, a retired civil servant was the LG while the security apparatus was headed by an officer of the Indian Police Service, S C Tandon, who was the Commissioner of Police.

A major portion of the Union Territory comprised urban areas while the rural parts were split into two tehsils—Delhi and

Mehrauli. Although by 1984 there were five police districts in Delhi, the entire city was designated as a single revenue district under the purview of a District Magistrate. Further, each police district was under the supervision of Additional Commissioners of Police, a rank at par with the Deputy Inspector General of Police in the non-Police Commission system.

The district police heads functioned through operational heads or Deputy Commissioners of Police under whom there were several Assistant Commissioners who were followed further down the pyramidal structure by Station House Officers of the rank of Inspectors who administered sixty-three police stations in the Union Territory. The foot soldiers of Delhi police comprised: Sub-Inspectors, Assistant Sub-Inspectors, Head Constables and Constables.

As early as 2:30 pm on 31 October 1984, Additional Commissioner of Police H C Jatav  received information that trouble had erupted in some areas of south Delhi where incidents of stone pelting and assault on Sikhs was reported. But the law enforcing agencies were focussed elsewhere and ensuring the seamless shifting of Indira Gandhi's body from AIIMS. Prior to Jatav getting information,  Police Commissioner S C Tandon was summoned at 12:30 pm by M L Fotedar (an important aide of Indira Gandhi) and V S Tripathi (a key member of the Prime Minister's Secretariat) and given strict instructions, which exceeded their prescribed brief, to ensure peace on the roads outside prime minister's house. The reason for the overzealousness on the part of the two men was because key members of the government—Home Minister P V Narasimha Rao, Cabinet Secretary Krishnaswamy Raosaheb, and Principal Secretary Dr P C Alexander were not present in Delhi at the time of the shootout. Therefore as a stopgap arrangement, the line of command was reposed in the hands of Home Secretary, M M K Wali along with P G Gavai and Tandon, but to little avail.

The attack on the Presidential motorcade was the first sign in a series of severe attacks on Delhi's Sikhs. Shortly after the

President drove away from AIIMS, there was violence in the nearby INA Market followed by more in the upmarket Jor Bagh area. An account from the report submitted by the Justice Misra Commission is self-explanatory:

> Vehicles of Sikhs started being stopped and their turbans were removed and set on fire. By the evening time mobs collected at several places had started stopping transport vehicles as also scooters, motor-cycles and cars either driven by Sikhs or in which Sikhs were found travelling. The initial shout of condemnation of Sikhs began to take a serious turn.

By the evening of 31 October, unruly mobs began attacking gurudwaras in central and New Delhi—areas under the administrative control of New Delhi Municipal Committee —viewed as custodians of Lutyens Delhi; and also in south Delhi where the city's elite lived. Evidence recorded by the Misra Commission established that thirteen gurudwaras were attacked after sunset on 31 October. Interestingly no "landmark" gurudwara was targeted by the mobs barring Gurudwara Rakabganj. This despite the fact that although vengeful mobs had specifically targeted Sikhs, they had spared gurudwaras steeped in heritage. Strange as it may seem, the answer to this may be found in the evolution of the political narrative in Punjab especially from the early 1980s when gurudwaras were—both rightly and wrongly—identified as the citadels of militancy. Although in several instances, including most famously the Golden Temple, gurudwaras were used as base camps by terrorist groups, not every Sikh shrine was taken over. Nonetheless, the decision of the mobs to steer clear of identifiable gurudwaras indicated the fear of the Hindu majority and a deep mistrust of the "other" which had crept into a city where Punjabiyat was ostensibly still a dominant trait...

# Two

# The Making of a Conflict

It is well known that every episode of political turmoil evokes different points of view. Most importantly, about its origin. Punjab was no different. While the insurgency in the state dominated the discourse from the late-1970s to mid-1990s, some experts trace its roots to a distant past and others to a more recent context in contemporary history.

By the mid-1970s, the issue of constitutional accordance of rights to Sikhs had assumed center stage and caused serious dissension within the community. Unfortunately, the period also coincided with one of the murkiest phases in Prime Minister Indira Gandhi's political career who was struggling with several crises on the domestic front—foremost being the Nav Nirman movement in Gujarat which swiftly spread to Bihar and other parts of India. This was followed by Jayaprakash Narain's call for Total Revolution and close on heels came the Allahabad High Court judgement which unseated her from parliament. Counselled by members of her coterie, primarily Siddhartha Shankar Ray, Indira Gandhi decided to take matters in her own hands and after a midnight parley, imposed the Emergency in June 1975 and arrested several opposition leaders. In Punjab, the Sikhs condemned her openly and paid a price. According to an Amnesty International Report of the period, out of 1,40,000 undertrials in Indian jails, almost 40,000 were Sikhs.

In one of his essays titled, "Punjab Crisis and Unity of India", Paul Brass, the noted professor of Political Science, wrote:

> Agitational politics are endemic in Punjab, used by the leading non-Congress party there, the Akali Dal, to mobilize support when it is out of power. It is especially significant to note in this context that the *only* sustained agitational movement against the Emergency regime was carried out by the Akali Dal during those years.

By 1975, the Congress party and Shiromani Akali Dal (SAD) had been political adversaries for more than two decades, when the state was still known as united Punjab and PEPSU (Punjab and East Punjab States Union). The Congress struck at the roots of the regional party for the first time, in a series of numerous others, when it managed to convince Akali stalwarts like Sardar Hukam Singh, Swaran Singh and Buta Singh to join the party. However the Dal held its ground and in 1957 even after its merger with the Congress, it was a Sikh leader called Master Tara Singh who revived the fortunes of the party and became its sole flag bearer. It was only later when the Akali Dal was perceived to be a supporter of a Sikh-majority state that the party's top brass appointed Sant Fateh Singh to lend a secular character to the party. Meanwhile, an accomplished lawyer called Gurnam Singh (from Middle Temple, London, who later retired as a judge from the Punjab High Court) was given charge of the Akali Dal legislature party, and he succeeded in marshalling the support of non-Congress parties for a Punjabi-speaking state. Although Gurnam Singh had strongly reiterated that the demand was non-sectarian, the division altered Punjab's demographics to such an extent that the Hindus were reduced to a minority. In 1967, during the first polls after the bifurcation of the state into Punjab and Haryana, although the Congress won more seats than any other political party, it failed to secure a majority. Consequently, Gurnam Singh became the chief minister of an Akali-led coalition, which was unique in character as it included both the Right (Jana Sangh) and Left-leaning parties.

It came as no surprise when the coalition government collapsed not only due to ideological contradictions but minor skirmishes orchestrated by Indira Gandhi in Delhi. The Akali Dal split but two years later re-emerged as the single largest party in the February 1969 mid-term polls. But Mrs Gandhi was relentless and struck back once again and not only triggered another split in the Akali Dal but also weaned away Gurnam Singh by appointing him the High Commissioner to Australia. Finally, her gamble paid off and in the next round of elections in 1973, the Akali Dal was squarely defeated by the Congress party and Giani Zail Singh was sworn in as the chief minister of Punjab.

During the four-year period of a Congress-led government in the state, it was to the credit of the Akali Dal that it not only functioned as an effective opposition party but also adopted the Anandpur Sahib Resolution (drafted by a sub-committee appointed to study the party's electoral rout in 1971–72) in October 1973. Ironically, the resolution which altered the course of Punjab politics ran into several controversies—in the initial years as a mere document for official records, which later became severely contentious. The noted political scientist, Robin Jeffrey observed how its adoption was viewed with suspicion and no serious newspaper in Punjab even considered it newsworthy. For instance, *The Tribune*, which categorically mentioned that the idea of the resolution was a later interpolation from a text predating 1973, which was mooted during a meeting in Anandpur Sahib.

During the Emergency, although the people of Punjab vociferously opposed the draconian ordinance and courted arrests, yet the non-resolution of two local issues—the transfer of Chandigarh to

Punjab and fair allocation of waters from Ravi, Beas, Satluj and Yamuna, remained paramount for them. Besides the question of river waters, the other was a more emotional and significant issue central to Sikh identity and pride.

Since the middle of the nineteenth century, the Sikhs formed a major component of the armed forces and during the Second World War, accounted for almost a quarter of the British-Indian Army. After Independence, when the government decided to freeze single-community regiments in the Indian Army and encouraged participation from underrepresented states like, Tamil Nadu, Bihar, Gujarat and Andhra Pradesh, it impacted the numerical strength of Sikhs in the armed forces. But even in the early Seventies, the community accounted for more than 15 per cent of the Indian Army and as a result of which the government was forced to put an embargo on such inductions from Punjab. The supporters of Anandpur Sahib Resolution perceived this as a challenge to the Sikhs' martial tradition and highlighted the Centre's bias towards the community. It would be naïve to assume that Indira wasn't aware of the resentment particularly when it raised ideological questions about Sikhs' identity and their commitment to Indian nationalism. Harjot Oberoi in his essay, "Sikh Fundamentalism: Translating History into Theory" wrote, 'perhaps no other "text" in independent India has caused so much contention and turmoil as the ten-page Anandpur Sahib Resolution.'

Two years after the Emergency, Indira Gandhi announced the general elections in which her party performed disastrously in most north Indian states and failed to win even a single seat in Punjab. In comparison, the Akali Dal's pre-poll alliance with the Janata Party resulted in the party winning 9 seats. Its ally won 3 seats while another seat—uncontested by both parties, was bagged by the CPM. In the state elections, out of the 117 constituencies, the Akalis won in 58, while the Congress had to contend with a mere 17. Prakash Singh Badal was sworn in as chief minister of Punjab but soon faced problems and from a known enemy, the Congress party which in its desperation to stage a political comeback, began promoting alternative Sikh groups to weaken the Akalis.

In *India's Democracy: An Analysis of Changing State-Society Relations*, Paul Brass highlighted how the Congress high command under Indira Gandhi and in cahoots with pliable Punjab leaders, obsessively conspired to split the Akali Dal and destabilised governments led by it. The first Akali Dal chief minister, Gurnam Singh was in office for eight months from March-November 1967; followed by Lachman Singh Gill who also governed the state for less than a year. Prakash Singh Badal in his first term, governed for barely fifteen months from March-May 1970. When Badal began his third tenure as chief minister in 1997, Punjab had undergone considerable political change. The Congress had lost power at the Centre and as a natural corollary, the Akali government completed its full term in 2002. But, between 1966 and 1997, the Akalis ruled for less than eight and a half years despite being elected to power and that sums up what Congress set out to do in Punjab.

However it is also a fact that despite its political eminence, the Akali Dal never succeeded in securing more than forty per cent of the popular vote; contrastingly, in 1980, the Congress polled better and garnered forty-five per cent of the overall vote. This was perplexing when viewed against the historical backdrop of the Sikhs, for whom politics was essentially an extension of their religious beliefs. Therefore, besides being a victim of Congress-led machinations, the Shiromani Akali Dal was never the preferred choice for the majority in the community.

If the Akalis managed to stay in power after 1997, it was because of their alliance with the Bharatiya Janata Party or BJP, while the Congress went on its own in Punjab. Harjot Oberoi in his paper made the following point: 'Clearly for some Sikhs, the Akalis had badly failed in translating the Sikh demography of Punjab into a permanent political power for the Sikhs.'

❊ ❊ ❊ ❊

In its original avatar, the Damdami Taksal was an innocuous outfit devoted to Sikh theology, and functioned quietly from its obscure headquarters in the town of Chowk Mehta, near Amritsar. But its transformation from a Sikh seminary to a cradle of terror in 1975 was the handiwork of an insecure Congress party which propelled the Taksal as an alternative to the Akali Dal and Shiromani Gurudwara Prabhandhak Committee or SGPC and unleashed its new leader, Jarnail Singh Bhindranwale on the people of Punjab. However, the Akalis continued to be in charge of religious bodies and swept the polls in 1979 by bagging 133 out of 140 seats.

Veteran journalist, the late Chand Joshi in his book, *Bhindranwale: Myth and Reality* wrote how the Congress found the self-proclaimed savant (Bhindranwale) suitable because he had initiated a campaign to 'cleanse Sikhs of impurities which had entered their hearts and was manifest in their actions.' The Bhindranwale-led thrust towards religious orthodoxy was in direct conflict with Sikh groups like the Nirankaris and it spilled over in April 1978 ( on the day of the festival of Baisakhi) when matters reached a head between the two sects.

It was the Nirankaris' annual convention in Amritsar where Bhindranwale arrived to disrupt proceedings and in the ensuing violence several people, including twelve Sikhs and three Nirankaris, were killed. The genesis of Punjab militancy can be traced back to that day in history when Sikh fundamentalism took root on the streets and spread deep and wide in the next decade and a half. In the immediate aftermath, it claimed the life of Baba Gurbachan Singh, the chief of the Nirankari mission who was gunned down in April 1980 by a Sikh zealot who later became the Jathedar of the Akal Takht. By now there was no doubt that Sikh separatists had laid siege to Punjab's religious and political institutions.

Meanwhile the Congress was unceasing in its mission to weaken the Akali Dal and trounced it in the 1980 parliamentary polls by winning 12 out of 13 seats and more importantly, in the assembly polls held after the Badal government's dismissal, it romped home with 63 out of 117 seats, while the Akalis had to contend with just thirty-seven.

Despite a spectacular victory, all wasn't well in the Punjab Congress as a war of supremacy unfolded between two Indira loyalists, Zail Singh and Darbara Singh. By now adequately skilled in the art of subversion, Mrs Gandhi made it appear like rewards for their lifelong service to the Congress party: the Giani was kicked upstairs as Union Home Minister while the latter was made chief minister of Punjab. According to Paul Brass, she was beholden to the duo because during 'her darkest hours in the Janata period from 1977 to 1980,' both Zail and Darbara had 'demonstrated their steadfast loyalty,' to the lady.

In a period of three years, beginning with the gruesome murders at the Nirankari convention in April 1978 to the killing of Lala Jagat Narain, editor of *Punjab Kesri* in September 1981, Punjab was faced with twin challenges. First, the palace intrigues set up by Zail and Darbara in propping up extremist elements against the Akalis and secondly, the unceasing violence between rival Sikh groups. A significant aside or development during this period was the re-emergence of Dr Jagjit Singh Chohan. A medical practitioner-turned-politician, and a former state minister in the Akali Dal government during the 1960s, Singh returned from the UK in July 1977 and succeeded in building a wide network of supporters for a separate Sikh nation called Khalistan.

Meanwhile, even as Indira Gandhi kept up the routine of engaging Akali leaders in a series of futile talks, on 20 September 1981 her government enacted a sham over the arrest of Bhindranwale for his involvement in the Jagat Narain murder case which led to severe tensions between the Hindus and Sikhs in the state. During the funeral march of the newspaper baron in Amritsar, some of the so-called Hindu sympathisers in the crowd challenged the Sikhs by shouting an objectionable slogan: "*Kachcha, kara aur kirpan, bhejenge inhe Pakistan*" which literally translated meant, "Underwear, steel bracelet and the sword (symbols of Sikhism), we shall send them (bearers of these) to Pakistan." The set-up over Bhindranwale's arrest antagonised the Sikhs in rural Punjab and left the Akalis with no choice but to demand his release. The government buckled and freed Bhindranwale in mid-October, a decision that instantly elevated his status to that of a demi-god.

Yet another significant event that changed the course of Punjab's political narrative at the time was the World Sikh Council (WSC) organised by the Akali Dal in the precincts of the Golden Temple in Amritsar. At the conclusion of the conclave, the then president of the Akali Dal, Sant Harchand Singh Longowal declared that if the government failed to implement the demands of the Anandpur Sahib Resolution, then a Dharam Yudh or Holy War would be declared on the State. While the Akalis struggled to stay relevant, Jarnail Singh Bhindranwale with support from Congress leaders, was given a rousing reception at every public meeting in Punjab's countryside. The Akalis retaliated and threatened the government to fulfil their demands by August 1981. A month later in September, a full blown "Punjab crisis" faced Indira Gandhi.

❈ ❈ ❈ ❈

On 29 September 1981, an Indian Airlines plane on flight from Srinagar to Delhi was hijacked to Lahore by a Sikh militant group called the Dal Khalsa. They demanded Bhindranwale's release in the Jagat Narain murder case in exchange for 117 passengers and crew members on board the aircraft. The hijackers were led by Gajinder Singh who declared dramatically that if "terrorism was the language of the 20th century", then they shall adopt it.

A day after the hijacking, the Pakistan army mounted a commando-style operation in Lahore and safely secured the aircraft. All the hostages were released and flown back to Delhi but the hijackers were detained and tried in Pakistani courts and sentenced to fourteen years imprisonment. Even today, Gajinder Singh and his co-conspirators continue to live in Pakistan and are on India's most wanted list of dreaded criminals across the border.

In Dal Khalsa lore, Gajinder is eulogised as a hero and a collection of poems purportedly written by him was released by the banned outfit as recently as March 2014. At the launch function, leaders of Dal Khalsa demanded that Gajinder Singh's name be deleted from the list of wanted criminals and he be accorded the right to choose his place of residence. The South Asian Terrorism Portal managed by the Institute of Conflict Management mentions Gajinder Singh as the manager of Dal Khalsa's official website designed by a group in the UK. In 2001, his wife, Manjit Kaur was granted political asylum in Germany and remains free to travel across the world except India.

Post the hijack of the Indian Airlines plane, significant sections of Sikh youth began viewing Bhindranwale and other militants as revolutionaries devoted to the cause of protecting the faith. The Akali Dal was further alienated and the deep schism between Sikhs and Hindus became evident in Punjab, Haryana and later in Delhi. On the one hand, while leaders of the Congress party engaged Bhindranwale in clandestine talks, in November 1981 yet another round of discussions with the Akalis came to naught. Barely a month later, Jathedar Santokh Singh, president of the "Congress-affiliated ", Delhi Sikh Gurudwara Management Committee (DSGMC) was killed by a rival. The deviousness of the Congress party was best underscored in K P S Gill's *Punjab: The Knights of Falsehood,* as follows:

> Bhindranwale stormed across the Punjab with truckloads of men, armed to the teeth, no longer with swords and spears and primitive 12-bore guns, but with sophisticated automatic weapons; no one challenged him. In December 1981, Jathedar Santokh Singh of the DGPC, one of his supporters, was killed by a political rival. Bhindranwale attended his Bhog ceremonies; also present were Rajiv Gandhi and two prominent Ministers of Indira Gandhi's Cabinet, Zail Singh and Buta Singh; they were fully aware of the killings in Punjab; of Bhindranwale's role; and of his presence at the Bhog. Yet they chose to attend.

After openly endorsing Bhindranwale and his brand of politics, the Centre made yet another blunder. On 31 December 1981, it issued an Award on the Punjab river waters without consulting the Akalis and this despite Chief Minister Darbara Singh's objection who was later coerced into withdrawing the suit filed by the Badal government in the Supreme Court on the matter. There was more ignominy in store for the Akalis when Indira Gandhi invited them for talks, a day prior to a crucial matter involving the inaugural function of the Sutlej-Yamuna Link canal. In the past, the Akalis had pleaded with the Centre that the proposed 214 km-long canal would not only reduce the amount of water for the state of Punjab but also divert it to Haryana and Rajasthan. But it was obvious that Indira was in no mood to listen.

Who is to know whether it was sheer coincidence or clever subterfuge when Bhindranwale shifted residence from his Chowk Mehta bastion to Guru Nanak Niwas within the Golden Temple complex just a week before his chief patron, Zail Singh moved into Rashtrapati Bhawan in July 1982. Punjab was reeling under one of its worst communal riots—heads of slaughtered cows were thrown into temples and in retaliation, cigarettes and tobacco (taboo for Sikhs) were flung inside gurudwaras. In the face of such extreme provocation, the state government was forced to take action, which it did albeit slowly. Amrik Singh, the chief of All India Sikh Students Federation (AISSF), described by K P S Gill as the 'striking arm of Bhindranwale's stormtroopers, responsible for many of the continuous succession of murders, dacoities, bank robberies and cases of desecration in the state,' was arrested. Consequently, Bhindranwale moved deep inside the Golden Temple knowing full well that with Zail Singh's "removal" from day-to-day operations, he would be unimpeded in pursuing his unholy mission and therefore chose a secure haven within Sikhism's holiest shrines.

The killings continued in Punjab throughout 1982. Apart from militant attacks, there were frequent reports of police atrocities involving young Sikh boys who were shot at random. The Akalis succumbed under extreme pressure and took the Centre head on by boycotting the prestigious 1982 Asian Games. The Centre retaliated by banning the movement of Sikhs from Punjab and Haryana to Delhi. By now it was out in the open: every Sikh was perceived to be an Akali and therefore a terrorist.

By early 1983, only Jarnail Singh Bhindranwale seemed clear of his intentions. The man held forth inside the Golden Temple, presided over judgements like a feudal lord and settled interpersonal and intra-family disputes. By December 1983, Bhindranwale was openly revered as a Sant or Saint by large sections in Punjab and he entered the Akal Takht, the highest temporal seat of the Sikhs. The head priest of the Takht protested but was ignored and both the SGPC and SAD were beaten into silence.

Before seizing the Akal Takht, Bhindranwale had claimed that the Sikhs had never demanded a separate state of Khalistan but if the government granted them the wish (as if it was a ripe fruit waiting to be had!) then they would be willing to secede. However, his stand was less nuanced after moving into the Akal Takht: 'It is for the government to make up its mind whether it wishes to remain with us or not.' By now it was obvious that the Prime Minister had lost her hold over the fundamentalists and the moderates had retreated far into the background. Eventually, Indira Gandhi made up her mind and began firming up plans for launching Operation Blue Star.

In January 1983, the Akali Dal called for a *rasta roko* or road blockade agitation in Punjab which ended in violence, killing more than twenty people. The incident found an unusual sympathiser in the then Chief Minister of Jammu and Kashmir, Dr Farooq Abdullah who was also up in arms against Indira Gandhi for allegedly attempting to split the state into two separate, "Hindu-Jammu" and "Muslim-Valley" regions. In response to Abdullah's gesture, the Akali Dal allowed its members in Jammu to hold a dual membership of his party, the National Conference. As was obvious in later years, this linkage created a further mistrust between Hindus and Sikhs. For example, when the Sikhs in Jammu came out to protest against the executions of Kehar Singh and Satwant Singh (accused in the murder of Indira Gandhi) in early 1989, they were brutally attacked by the local Shiv Sainiks and BJP workers. A report by Inderjit Badhwar and Vipul Mudgal in the *India Today* magazine (dated 28 February 1989) bemoaned that the day of the clash will 'probably live in infamy as one of the blackest days in the history of Jammu.'

In April 1983, the uneasy calm in Punjab was further shattered by a loud rattle of gunfire within the holy precincts of the Golden Temple complex. A S Atwal, a Deputy Inspector General of Police was shot at point blank range in the temple. K P S Gill wrote about the incident in his book:

> Such was the terror of those days, so great the demoralisation of the police—crippled and constrained as they were by the political leadership—that his bodyguards simply fled; the police outpost was also abandoned, and the policemen ran and hid in the shops. The shopkeepers pulled down their shutters, and no one dared to approach the body. The killers danced the bhangra around the felled DIG, and then sauntered back into the Temple.

Veteran journalists, Mark Tully and Satish Jacob in *Amritsar: Mrs Gandhi's Last Battle* recounted how Atwal's body lay riddled with bullets for two hours before the administration was given permission by the temple authorities to remove the corpse.

Despite the widespread outrage at Atwal's murder, several dead bodies were often discovered from gutters and drains behind the Guru Nanak Niwas where Bhindranwale camped. K P S Gill wrote succinctly about his experiences as a police officer in charge of probing Atwal's killing:

> This became a regular feature; bodies, mutilated, hacked to pieces, stuffed into gunny bags, kept appearing

mysteriously in the gutters and sewers around the Temple. The shrine, whose image can be found in every Sikh home, in every Sikh heart, had been transformed into a place of torture and of execution.

In many ways, Atwal's murder was the final straw in Punjab's alienation from the Union of India. On 10 October 1983, President's Rule was imposed on the state and Darbara Singh was sent home. Unfortunately, the dismissal triggered the first episode of targeted killings of Hindus when six passengers were pulled out of a Delhi-bound bus from Amritsar and shot dead by terrorists. This was followed by yet another incident a month and a half later and although Bhindranwale condemned the killings, it did little to prevent hostilities between the two communities. The Hindus cowered under fear and the Sikhs felt terribly isolated not only in Punjab but in neighbouring Haryana, Delhi and other northern states.

Meanwhile, in order to counter charges that it had abandoned all attempts to negotiate for peace in Punjab, the government invited the Akalis for talks. But the Akalis were in a non-conciliatory mood and upped the ante by raising a fresh demand for the abrogation of Article 25 (2) (B) of the Constitution, claiming that the following lines offended Sikhs because it stated that, 'the reference to Hindus shall be construed as including a reference to persons professing the Sikh, Jain or Buddhist religion.' When the Akalis protested by burning copies of the Indian Constitution, Mrs Gandhi's government retaliated by banning the AISSF. Sensing that the end game was fast approaching, Bhindranwale began fortifying the Golden Temple aided by a retired Indian Army war hero called General Shahbeg Singh.

Finally it was the gruesome assassination of Ramesh Chander (his father Lala Jagat Narain was also murdered by Sikh terrorists) in May 1984 which forced Indira Gandhi to seize control of the Golden Temple. A lot has been written to comprehend the complexities involving Operation Blue Star; if a nation torn asunder by insurgency demanded such an action; if the safety of a nation state was paramount when compared to the religious beliefs of a sect; whether Indira Gandhi deliberately ordered the onslaught to teach Sikhs a lesson etc. The renowned historian, the late Prof Bipan Chandra in a book co-authored with Mridula and Aditya Mukherjee said that the events in the Golden Temple,

> produced a deep sense of anger and outrage among Sikhs all over the country. It was seen by most of them as a sacrilege and an affront to the community rather than as a necessary though unpleasant effort to deal with Bhindranwale and the terrorists.

According to Ramchandra Guha in *India After Gandhi*, Operation Blue Star 'left a collective wound in the psyche of the Sikhs, a deep sense of suspicion of the government of India.' It severely impacted even the so-called enlightened Sikhs who altered their perspective about the events preceding the destruction of Akal Takht and most importantly, Jarnail Singh Bhindranwale who suddenly appeared benevolent when compared to the lady in Delhi. Ramachandra Guha has an explanation for this:

> Now, even those who had previously opposed Bhindranwale began to see him in a new light. For, whatever his past errors and crimes, he and his men had died defending the holy shrine from the vandals.

The deification of Bhindranwale, which began in the aftermath of Operation Blue Star gradually gained currency and became a phenomenon in later years. Elsewhere in the book there is mention of the Vancouver-based Punjabi pop singer, Jaswinder Singh Bains aka Jazzy B who sang in praise of Bhindranwale as he did for other Sikh gurus. Although severely misplaced, idolatory zeal for a militant is often synonymous with gratitude for his willingness to be martyred for the cause of religion. Satish Jacob was one amongst the last group of journalists to have met Bhindranwale, before  he was killed by the Indian Army,  and recounted the interaction as follows:

> One of the journalists asked him what he would do
> when the army came in. "*Aan dio*" (Let them come) and
> continued, "What can they do? They'll kill me, but we
> are going to give them a fitting reply." I realised what
> he actually meant—that if he surrendered, he would
> survive, but be forgotten. People would then say "*Banda
> nakli hai*" (He is an impostor). If he laid down his life,
> like so many of the Sikh martyrs, he would be immortal.

At the time of the anti-Sikh pogrom, the Punjab imbroglio was even less than a decade old. Although the state was taken over by militants in the Eighties and large number of Sikhs felt insecure and fatigued living under the shadow of fear, they vehemently rejected the secessionist voices of groups such as the Damdami Taksal, Dal Khalsa and Akhand Kirtani Jatha. They were also aware that the separatist movement was the result of electoral politics between local leaders of the SAD and the Centre led by Indira Gandhi in Delhi.

Eventually, Punjab was rid of insurgency when the United Front government led by H D Deve Gowda and I K Gujral, as the pointsman for Punjab, announced elections to the state assembly in February 1997 and the Akali Dal was elected to power. But the Sikhs still awaited for the Centre to dispense justice for crimes committed in 1984.

# Three

# The Horror! The Horror!

The sword, considered to be one of the most ancient weapons in history is nearly 5,000 years old. Legend has it that in India, its curved variant was made popular in warfare by Turkish and Mongol invaders from the medieval ages. Owing to Sikhism's martial history and Guru Gobind Singh's commandment to carry the 5 *Ks*, mandatory adornments for all Sikhs, the sword came to occupy the centrepiece in many Sikh households. Dr Swaranpreet Singh's home was no different. But the sword that was part of his family's heirloom was no ordinary weapon picked up from curio shops outside big gurudwaras or flea markets. It was gifted to his father, Giani Udham Singh by the Maharaja of Patiala in appreciation for his long service to Sikhism.

Shortly after midnight on 1 November 1984, Swaranpreet Singh brandished the sword while walking the streets of his colony as part of a vigilante group. The sword felt different in his hands. What had so far been a symbol of his religious identity, felt strange as a weapon of offence. He was troubled by a recurring thought: would he be able to put the ceremonial sword to use?

Wield it the correct way? Probably not, he concluded through the night and sighed.

That night, Swaranpreet Singh was extra watchful as there were strong indications of mobs approaching to kill and loot valuables from the homes and shops of Sikhs. While heading out to join the motley group carrying hockey sticks, hammers or just plain clubs, Swaranpreet had paused in front of the sheathed sword and walked out in the darkness flashing its cold steel. 'It looked beautiful,' he reminisced each time he talked about that fateful night.

For three nights and large parts through the days, this was Swaranpreet's routine—a hitherto unknown experience and in total contrast to a life he had known previously. The music of Pink Floyd, Bob Dylan, borrowed motor cycles and exciting rides with beautiful women.

Wrenched from his normal diversions, whenever he rested on a pavement for breaks during the patrolling sessions, Swaranpreet would be swamped by a feeling of being hunted by mobs whose voices wafted inside his colony during the day. On one such occasion, he thought of his mother—the pain, uncertainties and trauma that she had undergone. He wondered if he could suffer lifelong memories, and keep it hidden from his children, just the way she had? His mother was roughly his age when she had crossed the sub-continental border in 1947 leaving behind not just people and possessions, but an entire existence. Swaranpreet nervously thought about the tectonic shift and shuddered.

Eventually, Swaranpreet's career did change course and post October 1984, he abandoned his dream of becoming a surgeon and trained as a specialist in post-traumatic stress disorders. Treating emotional suffering became his professional calling and he worked with human rights groups, who drew on his experience with traumatised Sikh children in what was then termed internationally as "ethnic violence in Delhi". But in order to achieve that, he had to relocate to Chandigarh and enroll in the Post Graduate Institute of Medical Education and Research (PGIMER).

Like Swaranpreet, the year 1984 became a turning point for several others. The assassination of a prime minister was preceded and followed by political developments which led to a sharp divergence in what constituted the idea of India. When the Sikhs were singled out in the aftermath of the murder, there was a section that either condoned it or abetted it quietly. But as the outcry became cacophonic in the following weeks, these voices were gradually muted, but refused to disappear because they awaited for answers from an apathetic State.

Meanwhile for Swaranpreet, the trauma became a cobblestone in the narrative tract following the anti-Sikh pogrom. On the second day of the riots, his elder brother's wife began to get worried for her natal family's safety in west Delhi's Hari Nagar. In days when phones were a rarity, the only way to check was to make a personal visit.

On the third day of rioting (by then the Army had moved into several riot-affected areas), Swaranpreet cajoled a friend, also a local Youth Congress leader, to accompany him to Hari Nagar. Once he was assured of his relatives' safety, Swaranpreet and his friend became venturous and decided to take stock of various colonies that had been obvious targets of arson. It was either while walking aimlessly on a desolate street or perhaps in a corner—Swaranpreet failed to recollect the exact place – when they found a young teenage girl. It was obvious that she had been brutally and repeatedly raped.

The two young men covered her with a sheet-like cloth material and hurried to get medical aid but none of the hospitals agreed to admit a rape victim. The girl eventually died on Swaranpreet's lap. He was numbed yet again and his thoughts went back to the time when he and his elder brother had heard of the selective identification of Sikhs in Haryana in early 1984. As he looked at the dead girl's face, the aspiring surgeon realised how his worst fears had come true.

If that wasn't enough to force Swaranpreet to deviate from his chosen path, a ghoulish experience awaited him within days of rejoining duty. One afternoon, the police walked in with a sixty-five-year-old woman and demanded that Swaranpreet issue a certificate to declare her mentally unfit to testify as a witness in a case. It was obvious that the police were setting her up but Swaranpreet risked their ire and while proceeding to examine the woman, he began speaking to her.

The gruesome tale unfolded bit by bit... She was a Sikh resident of a west Delhi slum and lived in a shanty. Her son was a routine offender, but this time around, he was arrested several days before the pogrom, she said and had fortunately escaped the mayhem on the streets. A few days later, there were rumours that the cops had killed all the Sikh detainees in custody. The woman then told Swaranpreet how she had gone from one police station to another looking for her missing son, but to no avail. One day out of sheer helplessness, she began to lament loudly in one of the police stations and didn't stop despite attempts to hush her into silence. This became a regular nuisance for the police and they did what they knew best: put her behind bars.

Swaranpreet heard the woman in silence. She claimed the police had inserted a stick inside her... When he finally found the courage to give her an internal examination, Swaranpreet realised that she had been cruelly violated. That night, he gulped down a bottle of whisky to numb his mind, before sleep finally overtook him. The next morning, while nursing a monster of a hangover, he recalled how he had wanted to kill someone the previous night....

❀ ❀ ❀ ❀

Around the time Swaranpreet was walking the streets of Rajouri Garden with his family's ceremonial sword, Joginder Singh, a forty-five-year-old Sikligar* Sikh was huddled inside a claustrophobic room with his family and sundry relatives.

---

* Sikligars were a community of ironsmiths, bracketed as a Criminal Tribe under the repugnant British law of 1871. In the pre-Partition era, Sikligar Sikhs lived in what later comprised the states of Rajasthan, Haryana, Punjab, Madhya Pradesh and Delhi in India and in Multan and Sindh that became

Packed like the proverbial sardines, the adults sat in deathly silence and hushed the children into silence even if they made the slightest of noise. A "zero-watt", incandescent bulb cast a pale yellow light in the room. From a distance, they could hear a low buzz—as if a beehive was stirring into life. The undecipherable, low-grade atonal chorus wafted into the room and the terrified men and women knew that the mobs were approaching. They had come visiting earlier in the evening in the narrow bylanes of their Block 30, Trilokpuri house.

In one corner of the room lay a steel *paraat*—a circular utensil with a raised edge—traditionally used to knead dough from wheat flour. Joginder's wife, Surjit Kaur looked at the huge quantity of dough one last time before putting it away in the tiny kitchen on the ground floor. Even in the faint light, she could see clumps of hair stuck to the perfectly kneaded dough. A fan had accidentally been switched on by someone when hair from the heads and faces of several Sikh men had swirled into the *paraat*... Only Joginder Singh had refused to shear his hair. The others—his two sons, an elder brother and a few relatives visiting from West Bengal—had heeded the advice sounded earlier in the evening: 'If the Sikhs want to be safe, they better cut their hair and shave off their beards.'

Joginder Singh was firm in his decision and categorically told the others that he was prepared to lose his life but not his turban. Although he wasn't a devout Sikh, he felt outraged at the pressure that was being exerted on him to cut his hair. After all, he had always held a romantic idea of being a Sikh, or a Sardar, and felt a sense of valour with the turban on his head. Little did he realise that his headgear would send out a wrong signal.

But back then, the men used kitchen scissors to cut their hair, and while most performed the act on each other, the women were

---

part of Pakistan. Traditionally, they not only spoke a patois which was a mix of Marwari, Hindustani and Punjabi, but were largely unfamiliar with the Gurmukhi script. After Independence, a large number of Sikligars migrated to Delhi in search of employment and after staying in illegal tenements, were moved to various resettlement colonies in 1977 including, Trilokpuri.

also included in carrying out this emotionally distressing task. The trimmings could not be thrown outside the house, and thus lay scattered in the room. While longer tresses fell limply on the uneven floor, smaller locks flew and made the dough unfit for consumption. The group went hungry for three days till Army trucks arrived in their colony to transfer them to a nearby makeshift "refugee camp".

Trilokpuri was a little-known slum that functioned as part of East Delhi's underbelly along with its twin settlement—Kalyanpuri. The two were among several localities that were developed in Delhi in the mid-1970s and were termed ubiquitously as "resettlement colonies"; with houses built on twenty-five square yard plots, they were devoid of any civic amenities. During the Emergency, Indira Gandhi's overzealous son, Sanjay had taken it upon himself to "cleanse" and beautify India's capital city and the scum was therefore pushed away to the margins of Delhi.

Eventually, Joginder Singh and his family escaped the fury of the mobs in Trilokpuri because a man amongst them possessed a unique talent and used it wisely when the mobs came hunting. A clean-shaven Sikh who spoke chaste Bengali and manipulated the killers into leaving them alone! But if there was one other moment which took a toll on the family, it was when Joginder Singh's eldest daughter-in-law, Rani went into premature labour. With no medical aid at hand, the neighbourhood women stepped in to deliver the child. In that tiny room, with the young mother shielded from men-folk by a flimsy sheet of cloth, a baby stepped into life to become one amongst thousands, on a day when the lives of their parents were torn asunder. For some, this became a lifelong identity and for others like Jasmeet Kaur (see chapter One, Doomsday Delhi) who was barely forty-five days old that day, it became a millstone, a reminder of an incident no one ever forgot.

On the third day, dusk finally brought relief to Joginder Singh and his family. The loud and agonising shouts of people had died down and was replaced by loud announcements on megaphones—an authoritative male voice asking those in hiding to come out. The Army had arrived to rescue them.

But none of them believed the "voice", doubting it to be another ploy to kill them. Finally, when someone began knocking on the door and repeated the same announcement, one of Joginder's relatives crept down and peered through a crack in the door. The figure in silhouette looked like a man in uniform and they all filed out on the streets and huddled into an Army truck. Wafting across their narrow bylane, a putrid stench hit their nostrils. Joginder Singh turned around. It was a truck in which corpses and unclaimed body parts were being tossed.

Meanwhile, the truck that carted Joginder began its journey. Occasionally, it went past unknown streets; at times, police sirens wailed in the distance sending shivers down Joginder's spine—a fear of authority for those who lived in the slums. He still remembers the night of the rescue which had felt strangely reassuring. It was the first sign in several days that the State still existed.

Eventually, the truck came to a halt and everybody was instructed to disembark. The huge ground in front abounded with people ambling around aimlessly. Incessant announcements on loudspeakers assured them of safety and urged them to register their names and those of the missing. At some point Joginder Singh's mind went on the blink and since thereafter, he has never been able to remember the sequence of events that followed over the next several days. When he finally came to, he noticed that a few makeshift tents were erected over the vacant land adjoining the Farash Bazar police station in east Delhi.

By 4 November, twenty-eight makeshift shelters or refugee camps were set up to accommodate fifty thousand homeless Sikhs out of a four lakh population in Delhi. This meant that almost one out of every eighth Sikh in the Indian capital was forced to become a refugee in his own city. The actual numbers were obviously much higher as a large number of Sikhs had also moved in with their non-Sikh relatives and friends.

Of the many relief camps or shelters, the Farash Bazar police station in Shahdara was not only one of the largest in east Delhi, but also a repository of horrific tales as it housed the maximum numbers from Trilokpuri. In the anti-Sikh pogrom's official tally of 2,733 casualties, 400 were from this area alone.

After a few days at the camp, Joginder Singh slowly realised that in comparison to others, his family had been fortunate. They had only been looted of some material goods but there were scores who had either witnessed the killing of their family members or were looking for missing relatives. Every day, as he stood in a queue to collect food distributed by volunteers—young and old, Sikh and non-Sikh—who appeared to have suddenly descended from nowhere, Joginder Singh felt reassured. He was convinced that God had rewarded him for his unflinching devotion in his refusal to cut his *kes* (hair).

❀ ❀ ❀ ❀

Promises of a different kind were made by the sixteen-year-old Nirpreet Kaur. As a student of an English-medium school, Nirpreet often refused to speak in her mother tongue, except while reading the Guru Granth Sahib. She was the quintessential teenager who dreamt of a life with "and they lived happily ever after" endings.

But all that changed on the morning of 1 November 1984 when she heard that a mob was desecrating a few gurudwaras in and around her locality. By the time Nirpreet ran to extricate a copy of the sacred text, all hell had broken loose. A little distance away, her father Nirmal Singh was fighting a losing battle. Leading the forces against him, albeit stealthily at the time, were two Congress leaders—Mahendra Yadav, who later became a Congress member of the Delhi state assembly between 1998-2003 and Sajjan Kumar, a sitting Member of Parliament from Outer Delhi. Yadav was convicted in September 2013 after a long-drawn-out legal battle in which Nirpreet Kaur was one of the leading dramatis personae.

While fleeing her home (WZ-241 in Raj Nagar near Delhi Cantonment) in an Air Force vehicle sent at the behest of Wing Commander L S Punnu, Nirpreet turned around one last time and saw her dead father's leg aflame. At the time, the desire to seek justice hadn't taken root, she later told several courts; it was the next day when she returned to the colony to evacuate other Sikhs who had either been stranded or were facing attacks. Before reaching her home, she witnessed a mob that was, as she claimed, being exhorted by Sajjan Kumar, *'Ek bhi Sardar zinda nahi bachna chahiye'* (Not a single Sardar should be left alive).

The days and weeks following the ghastly killing of her father passed in a daze. Fortunately Nirpreet and her mother, Sampuran Kaur had the attention of a few influential people including Lt General Jagjit Singh Aurora, the 1971 war-hero-turned-founder-president of the Sikh Forum. In all the meetings with the General and his colleagues, young Nirpreet strongly demanded that cases be filed against her father's killers. But when Sajjan Kumar was re-nominated to contest the parliamentary polls in December 1984, Nirpreet lost all faith in the judicial process and decided not to testify in front of the Misra Commission. Instead, she swore to avenge the murder of her father and resolved to counter the system externally.

As a first step, she enrolled herself in Lyallpur Khalsa College for Women, Jalandhar and joined the All India Sikh Students Federation (AISSF). It was during this phase when she fell in love with a *khadku* (Punjabi word for a militant) called Gurdev Singh alias Roshan Lal Bairagi who was originally from the Brahminical Bairagi order of Hindus, but there is no record of what had motivated him to first covert to Sikhism and then turn a militant. In 1986 at the age of eighteen, Nirpreet married Gurdev, but less than a fortnight later, everything came to an abrupt end. It happened on the day the couple decided to visit Nirpreet's mother clandestinely in Delhi.

There are two versions of what happened thereafter. Nirpreet claimed that Bairagi was betrayed by an associate and the police later staged a mock encounter to eliminate him. According to the official version, he was killed after he had tried to escape in transit to judicial custody. In August 1987, Justice Ajit Singh Bains, a former judge of the Punjab and Haryana High Court deposed vis-à-vis Bairagi's eventual fate in a sworn affidavit. His declaration was particularly chilling:

> The Punjab Human Rights Organisation, which I head, is currently enquiring into the allegations of fake encounters in Punjab particularly since the promulgation of Central Government's rule in Punjab in May 1987. Our estimate is that about 1000 Sikhs have been killed during the past few months...Even some jail inmates are taken out of prisons and killed in fake encounters.

However, K P S Gill, the former DGP of Punjab and a man credited with snuffing out terrorism in the state, wrote in *Punjab: The Knights of Falsehood* that marriages amongst militants were often for sexual convenience or for upward mobility in the organisational ladder. In reference to Satnam Singh Chinna, chief of the (now defunct) militant outfit called the Bhindranwala Tigers Force of Khalistan, Gill wrote:

> He (Chinna) "acquired" a 50 acre farm in the Puranpur district of Pilibhit in Uttar Pradesh, and had a large kothi constructed at Delhi. He had killed half a dozen of his close associates when they had demanded a share in the money looted by the group. He had two wives, and illicit relations with the wife of a certain Roshan Lal Bairagi, another girl named Pinki, and a third woman in Mannawala village in Ajnala.

After Bairagi's death, Nirpreet Kaur returned to Punjab. Meanwhile, her mother was also arrested in 1986 for harbouring terrorists and remained in jail till 1990. In between, the daughter made her way back into the AISSF and after giving birth to a son, rejoined the militants inside the Golden Temple.

In May 1988, after the launch of Operation Black Thunder, Nirpreet Kaur—by then a Proclaimed Offender in Delhi—was amongst the first few to have turned herself in. I was among the group of reporters covering the event and remember the drama at high noon shortly after the first group of one hundred and fifty—including Surjit Singh Penta, a one-time athlete who had represented Delhi in national championships, but at the time notorious for the serial attacks in Delhi's Chittaranjan Park and Greater Kailash in June 1987—walked out of the Golden Temple. Four years and several bitter experiences later, Nirpreet Kaur's identity was sadly entwined with her husband's and she was counted amongst several nameless and dangerous women who had joined the ranks of terrorists. I remember her sitting next to Paramjit Kaur, the pregnant wife of Penta who had watched her husband die after swallowing a cyanide pill that he carried on his person.

Operation Black Thunder lasted for three days during which other dreaded terrorists like Chanchal Singh Udoke and Nirvair Singh also surrendered. Nirpreet Kaur was later arrested and jailed for eight years for terror activities and the woman who eventually walked out of jail was a far cry from the young girl who had fled home in November 1984 after witnessing her father's murder.

While Nirpreet Kaur was contending with a life of a surrendered militant, Mita Bose, a professor of English Literature in Delhi's Indraprastha College was embarking on a bus journey at 11:00 am on 31 October, accompanied by her engineer-friend and part-time activist, Swapan Lahiri.

The first thing that struck Mita Bose when she boarded the bus from the stand closest to her college was that it had very few passengers. By the time she realised that there were even fewer people on the roads, it was too late to get off. Like in the past, she got down to change a bus at Connaught Place, but was confronted with a bizarre sight of a black skyline with smoke bellowing from beyond the arcade of shops. The broad avenues of Delhi's best known commercial complex were empty; a few auto-rickshaws were ablaze and crowds in street corners were mechanically gawking at the spectacle and listless policemen stared vacantly at the goings-on. Every now and then shouts rent the air and a roar went up as mobs ran in one direction. Soon smoke was seen rising from that side. Occasionally, a Sikh ran across the street with his turban undone and hair hanging loosely around his face. Crowds chased Sikhs with shouts that sounded like battle cries.

Swapan asked Mita if they could walk the corridors of Connaught Place, but she refused and caught the first bus that came her way. She witnessed similar sights at the Parliament Street police station—policemen stood as silent spectators in the so-called revenge drama enacted in the heart of the capital. Meanwhile there were murmurs amongst Mita's co-passengers and soon they began to cheer lustily whenever a Sikh was chased and beaten up by mobs on the streets. An odd car burnt in some street corner and buses that had Sikh names emblazoned on their rear side, were up in flames.

A shocked and traumatised Mita Bose eventually reached her father's home in Chanakyapuri and related the agony of the bus ride to her parents and friends. She said a quiet prayer hoping it would abate in a few hours or latest by the evening.... But that was not to be.

At home, she was plied with an hourly dose of bizarre rumours picked up from the neighbourhood by a younger brother. That was when Swapan urged Mita to step outside the confines of her home and the academic world....

❀ ❀ ❀ ❀

Close to the time when Mita Bose was undertaking the macabre bus ride home, thirty-year-old Shanti Devi was drawn into the vortex of a chilling tragedy in west Delhi's Sultanpuri, yet another "infamous" resettlement colony. Tehal Singh, her husband, was a daily wage-earner and the couple had three sons and two daughters. Two of Shanti Devi's sons were adults and helped their father while the youngest, a "late and unexpected arrival", was four years old and obviously his mother's pet. The two daughters called Babli and Rajkumari studied in a government-run school, and helped Shanti in her daily chores.

Tehal Singh's family was part of a nomadic Sikh community because of which they had little or tenous links with either Punjab or Punjabiyat. But on that day, they were obligated into accepting the Sikh identity which so far had meant visits to local gurudwaras and offering prayers to Guru Nanak's picture in their window-less room. Shanti was quoted by a reputed scholar —who will be introduced a little later—for saying something illuminating, a sentence that encapsulated the sentiment of thousands of Sikhs in Delhi and other parts of India: 'All we wanted was to lead a quiet and peaceful life. We did not want to die for other people's ideas.'

Much like other localities, word was out that, "They are looking for Sardars… the women and children will be spared." Tehal Singh decided to go into hiding with his three sons and opted for a house that seemed abandoned and was locked from the outside. Although Shanti pleaded with her husband to give her the custody of their youngest child, he refused arguing that as a woman, she was feeble-minded and wouldn't be able to take care of him! Dejected, Shanti made her way with the other Sikh women to the terrace of a house close by, but sent word through one of her daughters, the ten-year-old Babli to reason with her father to hand over their last born. The girl returned without the child but was soon sent back because the women on the terrace saw a mob descending on the locked house where Tehal was hiding. In a few moments, copious amounts of kerosene was poured on the house and set on fire.

Babli rushed back once again and pleaded with the men to let go of her youngest brother but to no avail. And for hours after that, Shanti was numbed into imagining the agonising cries of her little child in the horrifying inferno. She felt let down by her husband and Babli who had failed to negotiate with her father and the mob.

That night when Shanti sat in funereal silence in front of the house that had turned into a smouldering cremation ground for the four male members of her family, little did she know that henceforth her life would be inextricably linked with Mita Bose and Veena Das, the world renowned anthropologist, who was then a professor in Delhi University. Mita was particularly drawn to Shanti's tragedy which was starkly manifest at the Rani Bagh relief camp that had sprung up close to Punjabi Bagh. On the other hand, Veena was struck by the Sikh woman's peculiar staccato style of speech. Veena later wrote in her book, *Life and Words: Violence and The Descent Into The Ordinary*, that the first few words Shanti said to her was: 'I want *sukh* (peace)—won't you give me *sukh*?' Initially Veena had failed to understand its import. Years later, she deciphered that Shanti had asked for death.

The reason Shanti stood out amongst all the female victims during the post-Sikh riots was because she had faced what most mothers dread: the brutal death and burial of a child. Mita Bose noticed how Shanti would replay the blame game in her head as a toss up between her husband's inadequacy and Babli's failure in retrieving her brother. The slaying of her youngest son was more than an emotional loss—it was also a cruel wrenching of the last male progeny who would have taken the family line forward. For Shanti, life with her two young daughters was of little consolation.

Her sense of despair was further exaggerated because unlike other riot-widows, Shanti had little prospects of finding a match in the emerging "marriage market" of *eligible widows* because of her age and her daughters who were yet to be married.

Mita realised that Shanti's tragedy was accentuated by her reluctance to become part of a collective trauma. There was also a time when she started believing what Babli had told her—even Tehal Singh considered her to be feeble-minded!

For close to a month and a half after the violence, Shanti remained a cause célèbre in Sultanpuri. Teams of volunteers who entered the streets of the resettlement colony every morning were made aware of her presence. There was of course another dimension to her tragedy—the monetary compensation which was closely monitored by her relatives. Although ten thousand rupees* for every deceased person was a pittance, but for impoverished families like Shanti's, forty thousand was a princely sum.

By early December 1984, Shanti took to walking the streets around her home looking for the remains of her husband and three sons. Every day before the crack of dawn when she went to defecate in an open park, Shanti would see pigs burrowing in holes that were aplenty. Every lump that the scavenging animals dragged out, Shanti imagined to be the limbs of either her husband or her sons. Despite a lavish *antim ardas* ceremony with a large spread of prasad at the insistence of her extended "family", she felt the souls of her husband and sons awaited deliverance.

Over time, Shanti was examined by several doctors, while Veena Das and her team of volunteers not only set up various forms of counselling sessions but also proposed to help her get admission into a government-run psychiatric hospital in Shahdara. But the plan was shot down by Shanti's relatives and neighbours who felt that she was faking her misery to grab attention.

One day, Mita Bose discovered that Shanti's agony had aggravated to catastrophic proportions. At the end of a long conversation, she pointedly asked the distraught woman if there was something she wanted? 'A sewing machine,' so that she could earn some money on the side, Shanti told Mita after considerable hesitation. It took a few days to find a donor. But on the morning it arrived, Shanti killed herself. Veena Das recounted Babli's

---

*This sum was increased by several instalments in the years that followed, most recently in December 2014 by the NDA government.

response to her mother's suicide: 'She found an opportunity "to do her work".'

After their mother's death, Babli and Rajkumari wanted to live with Mita Bose but their extended family protested saying it was inappropriate for young girls to leave home for long durations. The orphaned girls were obviously a potential source of income for the relatives—not only was the official compensation awaited, but also contributions from private donors after Shanti's suicide grabbed national headlines. In time, several Sikh families offered to adopt the girls and one even in Delhi but the family objected to the arrangement yet again.

After three decades of Shanti's terrible saga, little is known about the plight of Babli and Rajkumari except that the two remained under the control of the family for a while and one day everybody lost contact with them. In an interview with this author, Mita Bose regretted this the most because the two young women mirrored the lives of several women who may have survived the riots of 1984, but were trapped forever in a life which gave them little hope.

❖ ❖ ❖ ❖

Shortly before noon on 1 November 1984, Tarvinder Singh's father, the forty-something-old garment manufacturer, Joginder Singh died. Within less than twenty-four hours, his sixteen-year-old son, Kamaljit Singh also met with a gruesome end. In the years that followed, wherever she moved, until her permanent residence in the Delhi Development Authority (DDA) slum tenement in Garhi, also known as widows' colony, Surjit Kaur always found place for a photo frame encasing their pictures.

Surjit Kaur cried openly. Unlike most oral narratives which often lay emphasis on one aspect while diluting another, Surjit's story had elements of repetition. This "recorded" consistency was the result of having to stick to a single version because it was documented in official claims as well as in affidavits before inquiry commissions. Since several of these accounts were hastily jotted down by young volunteers, there were obvious discrepancies, a phenomenon common in several incidents of mass violence in which a personal tragedy is overtaken by collective grief and the seeking of retribution through peaceful protests.

It was as if he was *programmed* to speak, because every time Tarvinder Singh opened his mouth about that fateful morning, he began with how he could still taste the bread *pakora* that his mischievous brother, older by three years, had pinched from his grandmother's plate! The rest of the narrative, I noticed was not premeditated.

The morning carried no signs of an impending doom as Joginder Singh prepared to leave for his factory while Surjit Kaur readied his *nashta* or breakfast. Indira Gandhi's assassination on 31 October was common knowledge in the slum but the residents were oblivious of the trouble in the city until they were caught unawares and things began to alter dramatically.

Even before the breakfast plates could be cleared, and Tarvinder could join his friends for a round of games (as the schools were declared shut that day), the mobs had reached his doorstep. The gurudwara in the colony was under attack. When Surjit Kaur saw the crowds rushing into the Sikh temple, she recollected similar tales of violence narrated by her parents and others who had escaped the communal fury in 1947 and made it from Rawalpindi to distant Gorakhpur in Uttar Pradesh. The family had begun afresh and Surjit Kaur moved to Delhi in the late Sixties after her marriage to Joginder Singh. She wondered if the flames that rose from the shrine signalled yet another long march for her family.

The thirteen-year-old Tarvinder Singh belonged to a large family. His various uncles, aunts and cousins lived on the same street in Block A, Nand Nagri. The eldest, Jaswant Singh lived in the first house on the street adjacent to Ishar Singh. Joginder Singh's house came next and Balbir lived just a couple of houses down the lane. There was yet another brother who lived in the north Delhi colony of Ashok Vihar—where Surjit Kaur and her sisters-in-law had gone visiting the previous day—and as a result, his family had escaped the tragedy.

After vandalising the gurudwara, the mob armed with iron rods, kerosene and petrol cans made their way into the street. Joginder's family panicked and decided to split up in groups. Surjit Kaur's mind blanked out after this point in the narration. All she remembered and told various investigators, inquiry commissions and journalists was that she was with Tarvinder for the next few days. The two saw her eldest brother-in-law Jaswant Singh and his eighteen year old son, Jaspal Singh being chased, pulverised and burnt to death.

Surjit Kaur's eldest son, Kamaljit Singh hid on the terrace of one of the nearby houses along with some of his friends. Neither she nor Tarvinder witnessed Joginder being pulled out and killed but they were told by surviving neighbours that his end had come on the adjacent street. Surjit was unable to recall if she had fled past the smouldering body of her husband during her escape from the killing streets.

Kamaljit had managed to survive for a day till he was asked to come down by a group of men who were accompanied by policemen. As the mob pounced on him hungrily, the posse of policemen had coolly stepped aside. The final toll in Nand Nagri was more than 120 and the list included infants and young children whose bodies were hastily disposed off by an inept administration.

For the next couple of days, Surjit Kaur and her son wandered aimlessly from one location to another. They even stayed locked inside a dingy storeroom of a neighbour who drove them out. Later they found shelter in a police station but had to vacate it shortly. Eventually, they reached Nanaksar Ashram, a non-descript commune just off the Wazirabad weir on the Yamuna river that connected north and east Delhi. By 3 November 1984, a makeshift shelter for an estimated 3,500 people came up in the quiet retreat of Nanaksar.

Surjit Kaur was one among 107 widows camping in the ashram (there were more than 500 families living in the ashram which meant that every fifth family had a widow). At the retreat, Surjit found some of her other widowed sisters-in-law and forged a deeper bond with Raghuvir Kaur, whose husband Jaswant and son Jaspal were killed in the violence. It was as if the women were recreating the family they had lost in the bylanes of Nand Nagri. Later when the widows in Surjit's family were allotted alternative accommodation in Garhi, they brought down the walls between their rooms to interconnect their homes forever.

Of the widows who had sought refuge in Nanaksar Ashram, seventy-two per cent were between twenty and forty-five years of age. A further analysis revealed that thirty-three per cent of them were in the age group of twenty to thirty, a gruesome fact that indicated that the principal targets of killer mobs were the young and able-bodied male Sikhs. Nand Nagri also accounted for the maximum number of widows—forty per cent—followed by thirty per cent from the localities of Gamri (in Shahdara) and Bhajanpura. In the middle of November, volunteers of the Nagrik Ekta Manch or NEM (formed after a spontaneous citizens' initiative at the time), put out an astounding statistic that there were eighty-two widows below the age of forty-five in Nanaksar Ashram alone! Every family had lost an earning member and on an average had more than three mouths to feed.

Life in Nanaksar Ashram was a unique experience for the thirteen-year-old Tarvinder. At the time of his father's death, he was a student of class seven, but he had to drop out of school after he took refuge at the retreat. Soon, an entire year flew by, of which the first four months were spent in Nanaksar Ashram, after which the entire family shifted to Gurudwara Nanak Piao, the shrine where Guru Nanak had apparently camped while on a visit to Delhi during Sikandar Lodi's reign. By the time Surjit Kaur was allotted a house in late 1986, Tarvinder had turned fifteen and had not been to school for more than two years.

His mother and aunts were meanwhile busy completing the legal formalities for securing government-allotted houses and the so-called cash compensation which was grossly inadequate.

Initially, as mentioned earlier, the dole offered was as follows: ten thousand rupees for a death or for a completely destroyed home; five thousand for houses that were assessed to have been substantially destroyed or damaged; rupees two thousand for an injury; and one thousand for minor damage to a home. The women were also offered jobs in New Delhi Municipal Corporation (NDMC) as office helpers which meant a regular salary, perks and more importantly, lifelong pension.

Tarvinder drifted aimlessly for a few years and later began accompanying a *pheri wala* or street vendor who hawked on pavements. His teenage years were largely spent negotiating petty business on the streets and he gradually began earning a living as a fulltime hawker. A few years later, he bought a readymade garments shop from his savings and began life with his wife, Surinder Kaur.

'If life had given me even half a chance, I wouldn't have left school and perhaps even gone to college,' said Tarvinder in an interview with me. His deep-seated rage against the perpetrators was about the annihilation of an entire generation in his large family. I asked whether his children knew? 'Yes, and only too well. But I have ensured they do not venture on the path of vengeance...'

❉ ❉ ❉ ❉

Several kilometres away from Tarvinder Singh and his mother, life was beginning to take ugly turns for the ten-year-old Jasmeet Singh and his family. His father, Lakhbir Singh Virdi ran a modest shop, selling and repairing television sets in east Delhi's Laxmi Nagar market on a street paradoxically called Vikas Marg or "Development Pathway". His three-room house was a little distant away where he lived with his two sons and his wife Manmeet Kaur who was pregnant with their third child.

Lakhbir Singh's first response on 31 October was to down the shutters of his shop. As word spread about the violence in the city and smoke began rising on the horizon, rooftops of houses doubled up as viewing galleries. One particular sight was permanently etched in Jasmeet's memory: a thick column of black smoke advancing from the south-western direction of his terrace. And Manmeet asking her husband in a voice ringing with concern.

'That's where our shop is, isn't it?'

Lakhbir Singh was silent. He knew that his wife knew and so did the ten-year-old Jasmeet.

Fortunately for Lakhbir, his house remained untouched due to his non-Sikh neighbours who guarded the streets and tricked the marauders into believing that the Sikhs had abandoned their homes. A few days later, Lakhbir and Manmeet went to their shop and found that a large number of TV sets had either been looted or smashed to smithereens. Even the ceiling fan hadn't been spared and was lying unhooked and broken on the floor. But what upset Manmeet Kaur the most was a smashed photo frame encasing a picture of Guru Nanak that was once displayed in her husband's shop. She ripped the picture off from the smashed frame and preserved it for years before it was finally lost when her family moved to a bigger house....

As a child, Jasmeet often overheard his parents speaking about the financial losses but understood little except that they were unhappy. For instance, the thrashing he once got from his mother for demanding to eat a typical North Indian delicacy, a paneer or cottage cheese curry. It became more apparent when he and his brother were pulled out from an English-medium school and admitted to a Hindi-medium one in the neighbourhood. And then life gave them a reason to celebrate when a baby girl arrived in the Virdi family, exactly a month after Indira Gandhi's assassination.

Jasmeet recalled how he had never heard of Indira Gandhi till his father's shop had burnt down. But as a reminder, Jasmeet suffixed the year of her murder to the name of his kid sister, Behan Chaurasi or Sister 84!

❄ ❄ ❄ ❄

Around the time Jasmeet's father's shop was being vandalised, Meghnad Bhattacharjee and Kulbir Singh were on a train to Daltonganj (then in the state of Bihar) on the Chandigarh-Ranchi Express to attend a meeting of People's Union of Democratic Rights (PUDR).

A few hours later, the duo sensed danger. Shortly before Kanpur station, someone sounded the Phantom's Tom-Tom drum with a chilling message: "All Sardarjis! Please hide immediately!" Kulbir paid heed and hid in a toilet. A few Sikhs were pulled out of the train and beaten with hockey sticks. A Sikh passenger found a pair of scissors and began cutting his hair. Even though it seemed like the best option, Kulbir refused to follow suit and later recalled that he had felt safe in the falling dusk and waited for dawn when the train was scheduled to enter Bihar.

On the morning of 1 November, the train reached Renukoot, close to the UP-Bihar border and proceeded without any trouble. But at the Garwa Road station, murderous crowds brandishing weapons began pulling Sikhs out of compartments. Once again Kulbir ran into a toilet but failed to notice its smashed windowpanes. Someone in the crowd pulled him down. Meghnad screamed for help as his friend was beaten mercilessly. Even soldiers belonging to the Ramgarh Sikh Regimental Centre were dragged out and bottles smashed on their heads. By this time, Meghnad Bhattacharjee had passed out. After regaining consciousness, he found himself inside an air-conditioned compartment. The train was on its way to Ranchi but Kulbir was missing.

Meanwhile Kulbir had managed to break away from the crowd and ran towards the main gate of the station. To his horror, it was blocked by a hefty man who lunged forward to grab him. Kulbir then fled in another direction and jumped over an iron fence and faced a dead end. The only thing he remembered thereafter was how he had deliberately fallen on his stomach and somehow protected his head from blows.

It was dark by the time Kulbir came around. He decided to go to a hospital but instead staggered into a police post before collapsing again. Eventually some people admitted him to a nearby hospital.

At this stage, the Chandigarh-Ranchi Express narrative breaks up into three strands. In Delhi, word was sent to a pregnant Jaspal Kaur alias Pali that her husband had gone missing after being attacked during the train journey. In Ranchi, Meghnad had a nervous breakdown. He was traumatised for a long time and hallucinated about murderous crowds, and loud ghostly noises which triggered a sense of panic in him.

Kulbir was sent off to Daltonganj where the rest of his family lived and he returned to Delhi after more than a fortnight. But it was most remarkable that despite a life-threatening experience on the Chandigarh-Ranchi train, Kulbir never reneged on his commitment towards a democratic and secular India and remained steadfast in his fight for civil liberties. But, Kulbir was not alone in this....

A similar incident had left the maternal uncle of documentary filmmaker Teenaa Kaur Pasricha in a terrible state of shock. So much so that even after three decades, he refused to talk during the making of a film on 1984. The uncle was travelling by train in Madhya Pradesh and owed his life to a pair of scissors which he had hurriedly run through his long hair. The incident left him scarred for life and inspired a seven-year-old girl to tell the world his story through a film.

But a young army officer in the 80 Field Regiment was luckier than many. Captain Gurmeet Kanwal was posted in Kargil (Jammu & Kashmir) but often shuttled between Delhi and his base station in the picturesque Deolali, a Class I cantonment situated at 2,000 feet in the Sahyadri range of western India. Captain Kanwal was scheduled to return to Delhi a day after Indira Gandhi's assassination and boarded the train at Deolali station. But fortunately for the Captain, reports of widespread violence had reached the Army Headquarters in the Indian capital and Deolali was intimated to alert him.

When a group of Army officers reached the station, they saw the train pulling out. In a chase reminiscent of several Hindi film sequences, an army vehicle drove on a road parallel to the railway tracks and spotted the train in Nashik, a short distance away. The train halted at the station for a few minutes and Captain Kanwal was instructed to get down. He came back to Deolali and returned to Delhi only after it was considered safe for Sikhs to travel in trains. In 1984, Captain Kanwal's four-year-old son, Rahul was waiting for him at home and was later destined to tell the world similar stories on television as one of India's leading television anchors!

The stories of Kulbir, Jaspal, Meghnad, and their friends, in Garwa, Daltonganj and Delhi are unique. But none of them are linear accounts as they transcend to a much bigger canvas and become a bunch of storylines that form the lost narratives of 1984.

# Four

# The Symbols of Violence

Often, victims of mass violence crimes or genocide are tethered by a common hologram or signature. It was starkly manifest in the sub-continent at the time of Partition and reared its head yet again during the riots in 1984. But was the anti-Sikh carnage as horrific as the Partition riots? Or, did a new form of signage emerge in those few days of October-November 1984?

As evidenced in history, in most communal riots, women were treated as "fields" over which patriarchal societies waged conflicts. "Possessing" women of the enemy "other" was tactically used for appropriating the physical territory of the adversary. In the context of Hindu-Muslim or Hindu-Christian conflicts, women of the "other" were identified as "unattainable" primarily because of social prejudices in relation to inter-community marriages. According to the well known scholar, Yasmin Khan in her book, *The Great Partition: The Making of India and Pakistan*, sexual violence and the conquest of women either by abduction or forcible confinement, was an expression of an 'impulse to consume, transform, or eradicate the remnants of the other community.' Crudely put: within the framework of sexual politics in a patriarchal society, possession of women is mandated, particularly when communalism triggers social violence. This was a recurring theme in at least two of the most horrendous episodes of mass violence in south Asia: the Partition riots in 1947 and Pakistan Army's repressive offensive in 1970-71 in what was still East Pakistan. Beginning with the Great Calcutta killings in August 1946, even the Mahatma had strongly reiterated that women had been the "chief sufferers" of Partition.

However in the anti-Sikh carnage of 1984 (in which more than three thousand people were killed across India), sexual violence was not the predominant signature. There were undoubtedly several instances of rape—including one spine-chilling incident in Trilokpuri when an estimated thirty to thirty-five women were kidnapped to the nearby Chilla village and gang raped over several days. (A few such incidents have already been recounted earlier in this book.) Yet it wasn't used extensively as a retributive tool to avenge the imagined crime.

Without diluting the horror or statistics—essentially its absence—of rape incidents, it is also a fact that in comparison to women, more men were killed in 1984. One of the primary reasons being that sexual violation or the destruction of Sikh women was not synonymous with the overall opprobrium of the community. On the other hand, the humiliation of male Sikhs lay in something distinctly different. In more ways than one, their annihilation was intertwined with the politics that had resulted in their alienation from the State beginning the late 1970s. The action of Indira Gandhi's two assassins was posited on the community's male members, and the mobs took on the role of a retributory State to *punish* the guilty, while the government played the role of the silent spectator.

Viewed purely from a socio-historical context, the Hindus and Sikhs were culturally far more cohesive as communities when compared to other minority groups like the Muslims, Christians and Parsis. There was and continues to be routine frivolity, and strictly at a superficial level, best known to the world as "Sardarji jokes" but there are hardly any records of serious communal clashes. Although that changed in the early Eighties during the insurgency in Punjab and there was severe hostility between the two communities, the women were seldom if ever considered as proxy targets. Therefore sexual violence against women during 1984 was primarily motivated by brutal power and not because these women carried religious identities on their bodies. As was manifest during 1984, when the mobs attacked Sikh ghettos, they turned their attention on the women only after the "main job" of attacking and humiliating the males was concluded.

However, it was also argued that news reportage and public discussions at the time had deliberately ignored instances of rape against Sikh women and its use as a recurring tool of "revenge" mainly because the victims were guided by considerations of *izzat* or "honour" and either refrained from disclosing rape or described it figuratively. The other theory was of devious manipulation by the ruling Congress party in ascribing spontaneity to the carnage and thereby ruling out State's complicity.

The first argument has a past precedent. For instance, during the holocaust, it was noticed how survivors of sexual violence and their family members had experienced incredible shame in sharing details of the attacks, and carried the memories to their graves. Sonja M Hedgepeth and Rochelle G Saidel in *Sexual Violence Against Jewish Women During the Holocaust* mention that when faced with inconceivable horrors, women who were either raped or subjected to other forms of sexual violence, felt that their suffering paled in comparison to that of the entire community. Similar was the case with several Sikh women.

Secondly, the theory of Delhi's mainstream press downplaying the sexualised component of the violence, does not take into account that by 1984 the Indian media was full-bodied and had recovered remarkably from the censorship imposed during the Emergency in 1975. In fact, but for the accurate and bold reportage in newspapers, the most horrific episodes of violence would have gone unnoticed. At best, the media was often guided by some limitations, which I experienced in November 1985 when one of India's leading women's magazine, *Femina,* asked me to write a report on the first anniversary of the anti-Sikh riots. I was handed a brief for a story about the rehabilitation of women and children in the aftermath of the riots. I remember going up to the commissioning editor and asking that since there were several widows who had been victims of sexual violence, wouldn't it be of greater interest to understand how they had coped? I was brusquely informed that instead of highlighting the plight of a handful, it would be better to draw an overall picture. 'Why don't you do more "universal" stories!' And with that the matter had ended.

An instance of women's reluctance to report rape was brilliantly chronicled by the well-known feminist, Madhu Kishwar in a special issue of *Manushi* in early 1985, in the story of Gurdip Kaur, a forty-five-year-old Sikh woman from Trilokpuri. Gurdip explained why few were willing to report rape:

> The unmarried girls will have to stay unmarried all their lives if they admit that they have been dishonoured. No one would marry such a girl...Those women in whose homes there is one or more surviving men, cannot make a public statement because they will be dishonouring those men. I have no one left (meaning no male member). My daughter has also been widowed. She has two children. My daughter-in-law who has three children, has also been widowed. Another daughter-in-law was married only one and a half months ago and has also been widowed. I have nothing left. That is why I want to give my statement.

A few others also spoke out, albeit figuratively. Padmi Kaur, a resident of Sultanpuri who had filed affidavits under both the Misra and Nanavati Commissions, was one such:

> On November 1, 1984, we were sitting in our house. Our relatives had also come because of the marriage of

my daughter Maina Kaur. When we were taking tea, the police announced that all the Sardars should remain confined to their houses and nothing would happen. We got frightened. After some time the mob arrived, broke open our door and came inside. They caught hold of my daughter, Maina Kaur forcibly, and started tearing her clothes. In her self-defence my daughter also tore their clothes and also hit them. They tried to criminally assault my daughter. My husband begged them to let her go. The mob said that they would kill him, "*Koyi bhi* Sikh *ka bacchha nahin bachega*" (No son-of-a Sikh will be spared). They broke the hands and feet of my daughter and kidnapped her. They confined her in their home for three days...Now my daughter Maina Kaur has fallen ill and has become like a mad girl.

As is obvious, the two main factors for obliterating instances of rape were, a fear of rejection in the prospective marriage alliances, and the compulsion to protect family honour, which in this case ironically meant the necessity to hide the failure of their men in protecting them.

Apart from the overall failure of the State in controlling violence and its dismal meltdown in the days following the pogrom, there was complete apathy in recording cases of sexual violence against Sikh women. An announcement of a separate compensation package for such victims may have resulted in official claims, which in turn could have become the basis of an investigation and official statistics. In its absence, compounded further by a criminal neglect in providing timely medical aid and conducting the mandatory medical examination of rape victims, the women were fearful of registering complaints.

If we exclude sexual violence, then the three primary markers of the 1984 carnage—depending on the time of the incidents, emerge as follows. The first, involving sudden physical assault was at the initial stage; the next sign was evident in purely symbolic terms and became visible during the next wave of violence when the State's response was also tested; and the third and final sign, after an indication that it was State-sponsored, was most brutal.

The first signature manifested itself as spontaneous anger outside the All India Institute of Medical sciences (AIIMS) where Indira Gandhi's corpse awaited a political decision, which amongst other things was also about the subsequent anointing of the next prime minister of India. As mentioned in an earlier chapter, there were several instances of Sikhs being abused and roughed up, their turbans snatched and tossed away by faceless groups of violent mobs. The anger directed at Sikhs grew by the hour and there were similar attacks initially on the arterial roads away from AIIMS and later within residential colonies against people who returned early from work fearing reprisals. According to the Misra Commission report, by 5:30 pm on 31 October, even the well-known and prosperous Sikhs were targeted:

> The Presidential cavalcade appears to have been attacked by some persons out of the angry mob still waiting at the AIIMS and some of the vehicles were damaged by throw of stones (sic). Around that time trouble started in Jor Bagh and INA Market areas. Vehicles of Sikhs started being stopped and their turbans were removed and set on fire.

The anti-Sikh sentiment had a dual purpose: to avenge Indira Gandhi's assassination and to "unman" a community which believed in its martial superiority. After all, the construction of Sikhs as a martial race was rooted in history since the early twentieth century when they constituted a large chunk of the British Army during the Second World War. The industriousness of the community coupled with the Green Revolution in the late 1960s created a strong and popular image of a group which was peace-loving, prosperous and cheerfully boisterous. But as mentioned earlier, when the Hindus became victims of terrorism in Punjab, the Sikhs were viewed as a *"gaddar quam"* or traitorous community and this sentiment was magnified by the time Indira Gandhi was assassinated.

Since most Sikhs are easily identifiable by their turbans, it became the initial target for rioters as was witnessed during the first phase of violence when it was tossed and kicked away. Within a matter of hours, forcible cutting of hair and beard had begun, particularly after the police withdrew from the streets and residential colonies. This was the first step in an attempt to annihilate the Sikh identity. In several instances, it became the tool for revenge, while in others—as recalled in the previous pages of this book—it was used by Sikhs to appear "normal" like the rest. According to the Misra Commission report, this tactic wasn't successful every time, as was apparent in the case of Joginder Kaur, resident of Palam Colony in New Delhi:

> On November 3, 1984 when we were hiding in the bushes the mob came towards that side. They had torches and lights with them. They spotted us in the bushes and caught hold of us. I told them that we were Hindus but they saw the turban marks on the heads of my sons. They said "You are Sardars. You have got your hair cut just now."

Eventually, Joginder Kaur and her two sons escaped because of three policemen who showed rare benevolence and not because they jettisoned their Sikh identity.

The second signage of the 1984 carnage was visible once people began to return from their workplaces and were met with an indifferent police force en route to AIIMS. On 31 October and 1 November, the mobs laid siege over Delhi and other towns in north India, with a specific agenda of mounting attacks on Sikh temples or gurudwaras. This seizing of a place of worship had its antecedents in the history of Punjab militancy since the early Eighties, when in the minds of the Hindus, gurudwaras were terror bastions which was ultimately lent credence with the fortification of Harmandir Sahib or the Golden Temple in

Amritsar. The attacks on Sikh temples was to hit at the kernel of a community whose religious identity was bound by the Book and the physical structure housing it. In the long list of misinformation spread during the carnage, the most preposterous one was how armed Sikhs had assembled in gurudwaras and were planning an offensive. The Sikhs had indeed gathered in gurudwaras at a few places, but only to take refuge.

Interestingly, while large gurudwaras remained fairly insulated from arson and loot, small gurudwaras in sparsely populated colonies were severely impacted during mob attacks. The Misra Commission noted that, '...perhaps for the first time in recent history, such a large-scale mobilization against religious institutions of one particular community has been done.' According to a report submitted by the Delhi Development Authority (DDA), 180 gurudwaras were damaged in the capital, while eleven educational institutions administered by Sikhs were pillaged which included leading schools and colleges. In most attacks, several motifs of Sikhism were desecrated but most importantly, the Guru Granth Sahib and Nishan Sahib, the triangular Sikh flag which marks all gurudwaras and other Sikh religious places.

The third signature of violence which began only after it became evident that the police had made no efforts to control the first two outbreaks, was macabre and spread like wildfire from the afternoon of 1 November. Even in obscure, unrecorded oral histories, a repetitive narrative was the manner in which Sikhs were doused either in kerosene or an inflammable chemical which at the time came to be known as "white powder". More often, old tyres were ripped out from flagpoles and hung on to the necks of victims and set aflame. Interestingly, the common weapon of destruction was neither a dragger nor a sword, used previously in episodes of mass violence in the sub-continent. This death by fire method was in fact a re-enactment of a grotesque sub-plot, a typical Delhi-creation of the late 1970s and early 1980s—which by 1984 was commonly referred to as "bride-burning". By equating the martial Sikhs with hapless women who were burnt for bringing little dowry, there was total condemnation of the community even in death.

A sample of the ordeal faced by Delhi's poor and underprivileged Sikhs was first witnessed by a handful of journalists—Rahul Bedi, Jose Malliakan and Alok Tomar from the Indian Express group after they stumbled upon a horror called Trilokpuri where the maximum number of killings had taken place. On 2 November, Swami Agnivesh, who had led a group of peace marchers through the streets of South Delhi's Lajpat Nagar a day earlier, heard about what Bedi and others had unearthed and rushed to the trans-Yamuna colony late in the evening.

The Swami and his associates saw half-burnt bodies lying scattered like animal carcasses on the streets. While making their way past crudely-chopped and smouldering bodies, they noticed that several had been mutilated with eyes gouged out; some had burning tyres stuck on their necks, giving out a deathly and nauseating stench. Agnivesh walked through row after row of houses in Block 32, Trilokpuri and noticed burnt and demolished homes. Clumps of hair lay scattered on the streets, in doorways, inside rooms, on staircases and roof corners, indicative of a frenzied struggle between the attackers and the dead. Alongside lay several yards of turbans in various colours. This horror aside, there was the shocking realisation of complete police apathy and absence of other law enforcing agencies. In a testimony to the Nanavati Commission almost two decades later, Swami Agnivesh stated:

> For three days the city, its Sikh population was at the mercy of marauding mobs and received no help from anywhere. The destruction and killings were carried out with impunity—without any fear of intervention by law enforcing authorities. The victims' tales of horrors were proof of the depth of degradation the city had sunk (into).

The three signatures of the 1984 anti-Sikh pogrom were obviously interlinked. A section of Hindus who had either led, participated or condoned the attacks were convinced that the

Sikhs—primarily perceived as "guard dogs"—had crossed the Rubicon and should therefore pay for the transgression. The underlying message being the annihilation of their masculinity by using the least "romantic" form of death—to ensure that death did not accord them martyrdom; cocking a murderous snook at the lot who may have prided themselves for their physical strength, but fell hapless victims to a cheap can of kerosene and a matchstick—things that left brides hollering for their lives. From being an extremely proud community, the Sikhs' status was reduced to that of weeping wimps at the mercy of the Hindu patriarchy. It wasn't just sufficient to kill Sikhs but to ensure that even the survivors felt an acute sense of shame.

But the final denouement began with the first signature—forcible cutting of hair and beard and "untying" of the turban. This was essentially an attack on the symbol of *satsang* or congregation because by donning the headgear, one became part of a larger community. The second signature of the carnage was an attack on the perceived garrisons of Sikh power—it wasn't so much on the religiosity of the shrines but on the capacity of gurudwaras to secure both Sikh militants and those escaping the wrath of rioters. The targets of the third signature were essentially male Sikhs (the male child of the Order) who were regarded as "soldiers" in the conflict and also primary agents in carrying forward the bloodline.

In the several interviews conducted during the writing of this book, I realised that more than the inability to defend themselves in the face of a physical assault, Sikhs felt most agitated due to a sense of betrayal by the State. In almost every residential colony, the mute policeman was a reminder that Sikhs had been abandoned to their fate. The well known journalist and writer, the late Khushwant Singh and his wife Kanwal were escorted to safety by a Swedish diplomat-friend to the embassy premises. In many of his writings, Khushwant's empathy towards the Jews in Nazi Germany seemed exaggerated, but it amplified how even the affluent and well-connected Sikhs felt persecuted in 1984. Khushwant Singh's fate became a reference point: if a famous journalist with strong political connections had to scurry like a rat, what must have befallen the poor and ordinary Sikhs?

As an unfortunate albeit natural corollary, Sikh children became carriers of horrific memories and bore identities of a *dishonoured* community. In relief camps and later homes, where they were resettled along with their widowed mothers, children were often engaged in story-telling and picture-drawing sessions by volunteers. In most stories, the oft-repeated imagery for describing their tragedies was *aag ki laptein* (flames of fire); the sketches invariably showed a group of men surrounding a lone immolated figure. Seldom did kids paint pictures of mobs brandishing swords and bodies lying in pools of blood. Gory as it may seem, even they pointed towards what had become manifest at the time: the predominant perception of the 1984 carnage was enveloped in a ball of fire, and not bathed in a river of blood.

Universally known to be astoundingly resilient and astute when faced with injustices, the children gradually learnt to even *monetise* the dead while speaking to authorities. In retrospect, it must have been a dehumanising experience, but the children of riots spoke with a sense of pride while narrating their personal tragedies. In relief camps, it was common to hear ten-year-olds say, '*Unke toh do hee marey, par hamare ghar mein toh char marey*' (Only two people died in their house, but four in ours).

One of the most startling revelations was also in the uniformity of the method and tools that were used during the massacre. The manner in which the technique was replicated not only in Delhi, but in several other locations of violence, suggested a detailed and well-coordinated plan. Well known academician, Virginia Van Dyke in her essay, "The Anti-Sikh Riots of 1984 in Delhi: Politicians, Criminals and the Discourse of Communalism", argued that the killing of Sikhs were neither "ordered" by the State nor the government but pointed towards the existence of a highly criminalised police culture and the Congress party's strategy to politically isolate the Sikhs. She further elaborated that the riots had actually been 'organised for the government by forces which the government itself had created'; a situation that has often been witnessed in cases of mass violence against specific communities in different parts of the world over a period of time.

The late Rajni Kothari, one of the doyens of political science research in India, wrote how after Indira Gandhi's assassination, 'a relatively stable and safe place for the Sikhs like Delhi degenerated into one of extreme brutality and barbarism.' In the November 1984 issue of the *Lokayan Bulletin,* he argued that Delhi witnessed a, 'striking erosion of institutional safeguards against raw instincts and primitive conflicts breaking out in the open.' He further added that there had been a conscious attempt in the capital to build an,

> infrastructure and a technology of terror, especially since the days of the Emergency... What happened in Delhi in early November was not a communal "riot" like any other. It was instead a criminal hatchet job carried out by known perpetrators of lumpenized terror for which the terrain and the infrastructure were already laid out.

For a large number of people, 1984 was Partition, Act II. A constant refrain in Urvashi Butalia's *The Other Side of Silence: Voices from the Partition of India* was, 'Why had the history of Partition of India been so lacking in describing how Partition had impacted on the lives of ordinary people, what it had actually meant to them?' Sadly, even after several decades, there is no comprehensive record and data about the violence that followed Indira Gandhi's assassination. There are figures for the dead and loss of property but only for the city of Delhi.

Similar to the partition of the sub-continent in 1947, 1984 also forced people to change identities. Several Sikh families were forced to abandon their homes and migrate to Punjab as part of a demographic majority, only to live a life of *rejection* in their new "homes", an experience that has parallels with the Mohajirs in Pakistan. However, 1984 was still not as cataclysmic as Partition primarily because it was neither preceded nor followed by extended periods of communalisation like in 1947. Despite the schism between Sikhs and Hindus through the early 1980s, the carnage in 1984 was similar to a sudden eruption of a volcano that had no previous and long-running history of spewing lava. Although the stamps imprinted on the two episodes are distinct and there was an interregnum of almost four decades between the two dreadful chapters in Indian history, yet, the commonality of suffering, neglect and the suppression of truth binds the two intrinsically. Yet, 1984 was not Partition, Act II, but a distinct episode.

# Five

# The Daughters of 1984

The scene was straight out of a Hindi film script. On a certain winter afternoon, a short, stocky woman in her early Fifties sat cross-legged on a queen-size bed in one of the guest rooms in Delhi's historic, Gurudwara Rakabganj Sahib. This was the same shrine where after an episode of violence, senior Congress leader, Kamal Nath and the then Additional Commissioner of Police, Gautam Kaul (a cousin of Rajiv Gandhi), were accused of instigating a mob which had killed two people.

The woman was speaking on the phone with Joginder Singh, a witness in the case involving former Congress MP, Sajjan Kumar for abetting his cousin, Surjit Singh's killing in Sultanpuri. In July 1987, Joginder Singh had filed an affidavit before the Jain-Banerjee Commitee detailing the case.

In more than two and a half decades since then, Joginder Singh had swung back and forth during depositions: in 1992, 1995 and yet again in 2003. At times he turned completely hostile and denied (along with his sister-in-law, Rajwant Kaur) having witnessed the killing. But there were occasions when he stood by his affidavit and testified, most famously before the Nanavati Commission. Many suspected that Joginder Singh had been bought over which seemed unfair because not only was his son set aflame during the riots (but survived miraculously), even his daughter was kidnapped and never found. Subsequently, as a result of his inconsistent testimonies and also Anek Kaur's (another witness, who died in 2001) backtracking on her affidavit in 1994, the case against Sajjan Kumar and other co-accused was closed. Later at the behest of the Nanavati Commission report, the case was reopened for investigation.

On that afternoon of December 2013, Joginder Singh drove a hard bargain and it had fallen upon Nirpreet Kaur (daughter of Nirmal Singh, see Chapter One, Doomsday Delhi) to negotiate the *price*. Nirpreet displayed little emotion as she haggled with the man who had a dubious past. She spoke on the phone in front of a group of Sikhs from the United Kingdom, similar to the ones established in Canada and the United States to provide assistance for the victims of 1984.

Nirpreet wound up the conversation and it was obvious she had good news. Turning to the group of men, she exclaimed how it was sheer coincidence that the man had called her! The phone call, she added was proof that witnesses had to be paid.

The middle-aged Nirpreet was twice married. The first time to a militant, which was cut short by fate and the second time to a Non-Resident Indian settled in Germany, which had failed of its own accord. A fledgling entrepreneur, she had two sons, one from each husband, and shared an uneasy relationship with most of her immediate family. These and several other nuggets about her personal life were often grist for salacious gossip. But Nirpreet Kaur remained unperturbed. After all she was the star witness in the Sajjan Kumar case and one of the most sought-after activists in her community. In 2011, she had assisted the well-known investigative journalist, Harinder Baweja in conducting a sting operation to establish that money was offered to her by H S Hanspal, a Congress leader close to Sajjan Kumar.

As Nirpreet surveyed the people sitting before her, the scene unfolded for the umpteenth time. She admitted she was an important player in the saga of 1984 and how it had become imperative for her survival. But it had not only brought her immense grief, but hatred from several quarters, she said. By now she was ranting about her elder son who she claimed was in cahoots with some Congress leaders and was pressurising her to compromise by changing her testimony.

In truth, Nirpreet was not badly off. Her frequent interactions with overseas Sikh groups and easy access to the media had benefitted her as an entrepreneur.

I asked Nirpreet what kind of a closure did she want?

'The politics over 1984 is deeply entrenched,' she said.

What about your father's murder? I asked.

'Yes. That is my personal tragedy. I demand harsh jail terms for the accused,' she said.

The only time Nirpreet appeared fragile was when I asked her if it had been a wise decision to keep the truth away from her younger son?

Nirpreet Kaur had spent eleven years in prison for crimes she hadn't committed. She had even crossed over to the *other side* when terrorism was at its peak after 1984, but had returned and for several years thereafter mentored victims in sorting out legal disputes, even helping their children to pursue their education etc.

But she had failed to connect with her own children. The legal complexities involving several court cases had left her little time to be her son's mother. Then one day, at the home of her lawyer, H S Phoolka, she found a daughter in place of the son she had almost lost.

❖ ❖ ❖ ❖

Prabhsahay got used to Nirpreet Kaur just as she had to scores of women who routinely came and sat for hours with her father, H S Phoolka. As a teenager, Prabhsahay thought that her father had a job which involved sitting endlessly with distraught men and women wearing crumpled clothes, just as her classmates' fathers held jobs that took them to offices. However during the process of getting familiar with her father's visitors, Prabhsahay slowly learnt her first lessons in 1984.

In a way, her initiation had concluded well before her birth. It may be recalled that in 1984, the young Phoolka couple were forced to move from one place to another along with Prabhsahay who lived this narrative along with her pregnant mother. Yet for a long time, she had failed to segue the circumstances of her birth with the violence of 1984. It was as if there was a gap, deliberate or otherwise, in what she knew and understood.

Prabhsahay was born in April 1985 and grew up amidst stacks of files in her father's home in Rajouri Garden. After almost a decade and a half, she took her first decision about the events of 1984, albeit with little or no understanding. While embarking on the journey, she was reminded of her father's oft-repeated rule about the victims of 1984—the only way forward is to not get emotional yet keep the sensitivity intact.

In time, Prabhsahay became an accomplished lawyer and specialised in cases of migrant Sikhs who were denied visas by the Indian government. She told me how she had resolved to steer clear of the normal route. For instance, walking into one of the widows colonies to ask: 'Anyone here who was widowed in 1984 and hasn't been able to make a living?' And finally chose to litigate disputes under the purview of civil liberties.

However it was another riot in a different part of the country that finally awakened Prabhsahay towards 1984 and that being the 2002 Godhra riots in Gujarat. The fact that the two events were almost two decades apart didn't matter to her. Like several others from India's burgeoning middle class, the Gujarat pogrom gave Prabhsahay an opportunity to participate in protests. The deeper her engagement grew with Gujarat, the more disenchanted she became with Sikhs who seemed oblivious to the pain of Gujaratis. It was as if the disillusionment with one tragedy had led to apathy towards the victims of another ordeal.

There was a time when Prabhsahay wanted to be a doctor but changed her mind in high school and decided to study law. She told me she would often structure an argument within herself to justify her decision—there was too much wrongdoing in the world and someone needs to stand up against it.

Despite an excellent academic record, Prabhsahay didn't have a normal life that was so easily available to her peers. The reason was her unusual parents. They were not only victims of 1984 but also people who provided succor to fellow victims and hence faced security threats. Prabhsahay paid a price for being a Phoolka and her self-imposed exile, devoid of any outings even for pleasure, resulted in creating several differences amongst her contemporaries.

I visited the office of this young lawyer in South Delhi and noticed the benign presence of a few Ganesha idols on her mantlepiece—indicative of the *separation* from her devout parents. Growing up in the 1990s when the political muddle in Punjab had gripped the nation and religious identity cast a long shadow on Indian politics, she found great peace in the pursuit of spirituality and Ganesha, a "happy god" who placed no demands on her. As a matter of fact, her Sikh identity was never of paramount importance. She rarely went to gurudwaras and was open about marrying into a different community.

Yet this ambivalence towards an overt Sikh identity did not determine her stance on the carnage of 1984 or the legal battle waged by her father. On this she was in perfect agreement with him, who contended that the dispensation of justice cannot be solely viewed as a Sikh issue. It should also include the Executive's accountability, the culpability of authorities and a committed Judiciary. H S Phoolka decided that there must a degree of separation between his legal battles and his daughter's professional pursuits and ensured that Prabhsahay's involvement with 1984 was strictly focussed on cases involving the violation of human or legal rights.

By the time Prabhsahay entered law school, it was twenty years to the carnage of 1984 but what shocked her enormously was the ignorance displayed by her fellow students and a near obliteration of that part of Indian history. She also observed how this contrasted with the grim refusal by the Sikh diaspora to discuss anything else about India. Therefore, despite continuous offers to address Sikh conclaves abroad, both H S Phoolka and his daughter chose to stay away.

Over time, Prabhsahay had a more nuanced view of the anti-Sikh pogrom and was convinced of Congress party's complicity and later failure in prosecuting the guilty. But Prabhsahay refuses to lose faith and is resolute in her belief that justice will be delivered.

❀ ❀ ❀ ❀

Avantika Maken had an idyllic childhood. The six year old was blissfully unaware that her sprawling house, where she often got lost, was also known as Raj Bhawan or the Governor's House, in Hyderabad. All she knew was her grandfather lived there with her grandmother.

Avantika has vague memories of a clammy afternoon in July 1985 when a rattle-like sound had shattered the peace of her Kirti Nagar house in Delhi. She had just finished eating a boiled egg and wondered about the noise because Diwali, the festival of lights, was still several months away. She ran outside and witnessed a horrifying sight. Her father Lalit Maken and mother, Geetanjali lay dying in a pool of blood. They were shot by three men who fled on a scooter after ascertaining that the job had been done. A report in *The Telegraph* newspaper recapitulated the event lucidly:

> As Avantika turned, she saw her father Lalit Maken, then MP from South Delhi, lying still in a pool of blood next to a security guard, who was also motionless. Terrified and confused, she ran back to her mother, crying and screaming. But by then, Geetanjali's face too had become calm and still.

The murder of Avantika's father was the result of a terse, four-line paragraph in a booklet titled, "Who Are The Guilty?" (see chapter Eight, The Citizens Collective) in which he was identified as a provocateur by survivors of the anti-sikh riots:

> Lalit (Maken), Cong. (I) Trade Union Leader and Metropolitan Councillor. Reportedly paid to mob Rs. 100 each plus a bottle of liquor. A white ambassador car reportedly belonging to him came 4 times to the G.T. Road area near Azadpur. Instructions to mobs indulging in arson were given from inside the car.

In November 1985, Dr Shankar Dayal Sharma was appointed the Governor of Punjab and moved to Chandigarh. Less than a year later, it was time to move again—this time to Mumbai to take up the governorship of Maharashtra. A year and a half later, he moved back to Delhi and took over as India's Vice President. A sprawling bungalow on Delhi's Maulana Azad Road, adjacent to the Vigyan Bhawan was home to the bubbly girl who was tormented by dark images of her parents lying in a pool of fresh blood. Five years later, in 1992, it was time for another move: this time to the massive complex atop the Raisina Hill, also called the Rashtrapati Bhawan or the President's Estate. By the time Avantika was twelve, life had meant five changes of residence and as many set of friends.

In another part of the world, life-changing events were impacting Ranjit Singh "Kuki" Gill. While Avantika was meandering her way through the maze of rooms in what had once been the Viceroy's House in British India, Gill was in a United States prison awaiting the resolution of extradition proceedings by the Indian government in February 1988.

Gill's journey into the netherworld began on India's Independence Day in 1984 after he had declined to pursue a PhD programme in Kansas University (he already had a

Masters in plant breeding from the Punjab Agricultural University, Ludhiana). Instead he decided to get baptised for the *quam,* which in the aftermath of Operation Blue Star meant keeping the flag of militancy flying—if not in deed, then at least in thought. The decision to serve the Order stemmed from a deep-seated angst after he was arrested by the police on the flimsy charge of wearing a black turban. A few days after this incident, Kuki joined the All Indian Sikh Students Federation or AISSF. In contrast, his two siblings were studying medicine and his father, Khem Singh Gill, was a senior professor in the university and later went on to become its Vice Chancellor and was also awarded the Padma Bhushan. Ironically, the professor received the award in the same year Avantika moved back to Delhi with her grandparents. But it was still time before the two families became familiar with each other.

Kuki Gill was one among hundreds of fugitives who had fled India using forged papers after the riots in 1984. In 1985, he was charged with the murder of the Maken couple along with Sukhdev Singh alias Sukha and Harjinder Singh aka Jinda. On 28 February 1986, Kuki fled to the United States but was detained by the Interpol on 14 May 1987 after it issued a lookout notice in his name following India's plea.

Meanwhile Sukha and Jinda carried out two more assassinations—Arjan Dass in September 1985 (a Congress leader named in the People's Union of Civil Liberties or PUCL report), and General Arun Vaidya, chief of the Indian Army at the time of Operation Blue Star, in January 1986. The two were later arrested and executed–exactly three months after Avantika moved into the President's Estate with her grandparents.

By the time Kuki was finally extradited to India on 7 May 2000, Avantika was a young woman and had moved out of Rashtrapati Bhawan at the end of her grandfather's tenure as President of India. She was also preparing for her betrothal to an Indian Air Force officer, which eventually ended on a sour note. Meanwhile, Kuki prepared for a long haul in Indian jails despite an assurance that he would not be charged under the now-defunct Terrorist and Disruptive Activities (Prevention) Act, or TADA and would instead be tried for the offences of murder and attempt to murder.

❖ ❖ ❖ ❖

In May 2004, Avantika encountered the surviving assassin of her parents. The meeting was set up by a young man whose father, Dr D N Tewari was a member of the Rajya Sabha and was shot dead in April 1984 by terrorists in Chandigarh. The son was at the time Vice President of his college union besides being the general secretary of the National Students Union of India (NSUI). This young man called, Manish Tewari  later went on become the Union Minister for Information and Broadcasting in Dr Manmohan Singh's government.

A report in the *Open* magazine in June 2009 described the meeting that brought Avantika face-to-face with Kuki, who was then an undertrial:

> Kuki recalls it vividly. 'I had gone alone to meet her. As soon as we sat down, she asked me "Why?" I answered. After all, it did not matter who had carried out the act. I told her there was nothing personal about it. It was a result of the turn of events. As a Sikh, I was on one side, and she, despite being Punjabi, as a Hindu was on the other side. If Darbar Sahib had not been attacked, if the riots had not taken place, none of this would have happened.'

Avantika wanted to know the exact motive behind her father's murder. Kuki replied matter of factly: because his name was on the *list*. She however refrained from asking about her mother's killing. But Kuki decided to tell her. It was a mistake, he conceded. When Lalit Maken ran inside after being shot, Geetanjali came out to embrace him and it was typical collateral damage. He explained further—just as innocent Sikhs were killed in an act of vengeance for an assassination they were never part of, or for a war which was never theirs! Avantika was severely impacted after meeting Kuki but the moment soon turned over and she was back to addressing more pressing matters in her life.

This included seeking the assistance of Congress President, Sonia Gandhi or rather, benefitting from her intervention. For some time now, a young man called Ashok Tanwar (who was a general secretary of the NSUI), had been pursuing her for marriage. Finally, Sonia Gandhi cajoled her and Avantika, who had a daughter from the failed marriage, married Ashok in June 2005. It would take another four years before Kuki's long trial came to an end in which he was pronounced guilty and awarded a life sentence. But the then chief minister of Delhi, Sheila Dikshit invoked her powers to commute his sentence after she had Avantika's consent, a decision that was gently aided by her uncle Ajay Maken, another senior Congress leader and a former union minister. The final order that enabled Kuki to walk out of jail was issued on 7 July 2009.

What had made the daughter pardon the man guilty of assassinating her parents? What could have led to a change of heart? Was her act a silent admission from a leading political family of involvement in the carnage of 1984? Or was it more philosophical? These questions remain unanswered despite several efforts by journalists and one even by filmmaker Mahesh Bhatt, who proposed a film on Avantika's life, but to no avail.

❀ ❀ ❀ ❀

I tracked Kuki down to Ludhiana and was surprised to see him filing stories for a London-based website, and a radio station in Toronto between tending to his agricultural land. His wife, Harabhjyot Kaur is thirteen years younger and at fifty-three, he is father to a four-year-old daughter called, Gneeve. His email ID is suffixed with an interesting number, 2004 and I asked him why? 'That is the year when I tasted freedom after a long detention in the US,' he said.

I asked him if he felt any remorse? He spoke about his gratitude to Avantika, but reiterated that 1984–85 should be analysed in the historical context. 'I would have done things differently... perhaps sublimated my anger, understood the political process involving Punjab,' he said calmly. During the conversation, I noticed that it caused him great discomfort when queried specifically about 1984: why did the government allow the Golden Temple to be converted into a veritable fortress? What was the need for a "botched up" army operation etc?

'I go to sleep every night wondering if truth shall ever be told?' Kuki said. But any fresh initiative in the political process still makes him hopeful and he dreams of becoming a part of it. It happened even as recently as the spring of 2011 after the emergence of the Aam Aadmi Party (AAP) which initiated some steps to bring a closure to the anti-Sikh riots of 1984.

Since his acquittal, Kuki has never felt the need to meet Avantika. It was as if the chord which bound them together had finally come undone.

❀ ❀ ❀ ❀

Children become aware of the world around them in various ways, including the names they are taught to use while addressing others. They also start responding to any name, however absurd, when others begin using it regularly. Even as a baby, Gurpreet Kaur knew instinctively that there was something unusual about her name.

During the writing of this book, it became evident that even after a quarter of a century she wasn't ready to discuss her past and particularly after what I'd discovered. When Jasmeet Singh began calling Gurpreet, Behan Chaurasi, she thought this was yet another name for her besides Nanni (the little one) that her parents lovingly used. It was only after she began going to the neighbourhood Hindi-medium school  and learnt the number tables, that she realized that a part of her name was in fact a number!

She then asked her mother and when that yielded no response, Gurpreet presumed it had to do with the year of her birth.

Around this time, it was on a Sunday when her father was cleaning out a cupboard that a few old photographs tumbled out and scattered on the floor. In that lot was a typical studio shot—a picture of a young Sardar Lakhbir Singh Virdi and his wife, Manmeet Kaur, dressed in their best finery with their two sons on their laps. The elder Jasmeet on his father's right knee and the younger Harmeet clinging on to his mother, looking intently into the camera. Gurpreet Kaur wanted to know why she wasn't part of the family picture? 'You weren't born yet!' said her father.

The little girl pranced around and picked up yet another photograph of a burnt shop and asked her father about it. Manmeet stared at her husband as he told their daughter about the incident. The little girl wanted to know what riots meant and why was their shop burnt? The father faltered at first but explained the entire sequence of events to her. Gurpreet understood that some people had attacked Sikhs and many had died in the violence. However she still did not correlate 1984 with her name!

It took her a few years before she could finally establish a connection with the stories her mother narrated about those terrible days in Delhi when there was smoke all around. Even as the little girl swam in a sea of stories which were often gory, she slowly learnt the truth about those riotous days and nights. For instance, how her family was evacuated by their domestic servant and took refuge in her house before there was normalcy.

Gurpreet was studying in Khalsa Girls School in Daryaganj (the family could no longer afford to send their children to private, English-medium schools and opted for those run by Sikh bodies) and developed an aversion for her name. Whenever she argued with Jasmeet, he would tease her by saying it was because she was born just a month after their shop was burnt. And if Gurpreet retaliated more aggressively, he would taunt her by calling her Indira Gandhi! On the surface, it seemed like regular sibling banter but Gurpreet carried a deep-seated guilt of being the harbinger of misfortune for her family. The mother tried reasoning with her that the family had survived only because she had arrived a few weeks after the carnage. Yet the pain remained with her for long and it took her more than a decade to laugh at her unusual nickname.

The child in Gurpreet obviously understood little of politics but grew up with an intense hatred for the deceased prime minister and her son, Sanjay Gandhi. Over time she was convinced that if the events of 1984 were to recur, she would take the lead in retaliating against the enemies. She would often fantasise about chasing a mob and wielding the baton like a policewoman but that was not to be, because she had consciously chosen to underperform academically lest she became an economic burden for her father. In my meeting with her, I sensed how Gurpreet rationalised her failure. 'My family would have never allowed me to become a cop, so there was no point working hard for it,' she said.

It was this sense of outrage, tucked carefully away in the deep recesses of her mind that impelled her to convert to an *amritdhari* Sikh, just a month before her wedding. Her parents had already tasted the *"amrit"* or nectar of baptism after the riots in 1984 and their daughter followed suit to reinforce their Sikh identity.

The decision of the Virdi family to become devout Sikhs was also reflected in the community's political belief that the Congress party will not be granted reprieve. It became apparent when I met them in the run-up to the 2014 general elections. The entire family had decided to vote for the Narendra Modi-led BJP as an endorsement for the man and not necessarily his party.

❀ ❀ ❀ ❀

At a certain point in her life, Jasmeet Kaur whom we met in the previous pages, became Gurpreet Kaur's sister-in-law after she married her brother, Harmeet Singh. Both the women were born in 1984 and witnessed the riots but those were mere coincidences.

They were completely different personalities; Gurpreet was extroverted, while her sister-in-law kept to herself.

Jasmeet Kaur was clearly paranoid. The initial fears took root at the time of her birth but the memories lasted because of the constant buzz around her: tales of how her maternal grandparents had been targeted in Gurgaon during her first visit to their home as an infant. Like Behan Chaurasi, she was convinced about her ill-fated birth.

Even her marriage to Harmeet didn't help. Although her husband had fleeting memories of 1984 as a nine-year-old, he didn't notice his wife's reticence. Till the time she came out and spoke about her fears, no one in the family had an inkling about her ailment and presumed she was a recluse. Then one day she decided to break her silence and said profoundly, 'Let not thousands of other girls who may have undergone similar experiences live with a fear in their hearts and silence on their lips.'

Amongst several other reasons, the tragedies of the two young women was compounded due to a sense of isolation. In the past three decades, the two were faced with numerous instances when the families—both natal and marital—would be confronted with a 1984-related development and express anguish and extreme anger. But as girls and later women, Gurpreet and Jasmeet occupied the lower end of the hierarchy and were forced to keep quiet in the absence of an audience.

Eventually the society will become poorer as no record of such narratives will survive. Only the headline news will linger on, till of course a more astounding one takes over.

❈ ❈ ❈ ❈

Although the daughters of 1984 are inexorably linked to those few days in November 1984, some opted to live with the memories, while others extricated themselves. Nirpreet Kaur struggled with a complicated personal life in order to overcome her sense of angst; Prabhsahay Kaur ploughed the system from within because she believed in change; Gurpreet Kaur and Jasmeet Kaur found few avenues to articulate their concerns. Only a rare one like Safina Uberoi was able to exorcise her fears by lending a creative edge to her personal experiences and recast them to develop a better understanding of what assailed India and its people during those days. Safina was fortunate only because of her enlightened parents who consciously raised their children in a liberal world.

For most part of a year, Safina lives in Australia but often returns to make films, meet people, take care of her parents and most importantly, to dream. Our paths crossed on one such occasion and we reminisced about events that bound us together, despite the distance. That was in the immediate aftermath of 1984 when Safina and her mother, Patricia would spend hours at Delhi's refugee camps and I would too at a distant another. They distributed sanitary napkins, helped feed people and recorded testimonies. In her films she describes her emotions as follows:

> I wanted the camps to go on and on so that I could assuage the terrible guilt of having survived. But eventually the camps were disbanded. People went home to rebuild their lives. And, I learnt a very important thing: Even the most terrible wound can begin to heal.

# Six

# The Lost Turban

Wing Commander Randhir Singh Chhatwal was not only the oldest, but the only Sikh in the group that alighted from a mini-bus. Although his other co-passengers were even a couple of years younger than his two sons, they displayed great fortitude and escorted Chhatwal to the edge of a sprawling ground.

The vast expanse was teeming with Sikhs. Chhatwal noticed several make-shift tents pitched on the flanks and a few children playing catch with a ball in the middle of the ground. Soon, he and the mini-bus group were surrounded by a crowd which began shouting in a chorus. Chhatwal took a while to understand that they were complaining about the lack of food and blankets to cover them at night. He noticed a middle-aged woman speaking to a few men in groups of ones and twos. Her name was Jaya Jaitley who along with a small group of volunteers was there to provide relief for victims of the anti-Sikh pogrom.

It was a few hours since Chhatwal had arrived at the south Delhi-situated Lajpat Bhawan, cheek-by-jowl Vikram Hotel, a mid-size place beginning to go past its best days. He had read about it in the newspapers but was completely taken aback by the reality of  the situation. Hundreds of people were engaged in a flurry of activities; a small group was loading stuff into a truck; he could make out sacks of wheat flour, pulses, vegetable oil, spices and condiments stacked in one corner. Thousands of warm blankets lay in stacks and were readied for distribution. Chhatwal hesitatingly approached a person, who appeared to carry a sense of authority and enquired if there was an office where he could report and enlist for relief work? The retired Air Force officer was ushered into a room where he began to explain the purpose of his visit and was almost cut short. It was obvious that there was no time for standing on such ceremonies.

Chhatwal was instructed to join the team heading for Farash Bazar in Shahdara, one of Delhi's oldest colonies across the Yamuna. By the time the mini-bus rattled to a stop an hour later, Chhatwal learnt that Farash Bazar was the biggest relief camp in east Delhi.

On reaching, Chhatwal was more distressed to see large number of Sikhs with bizarre haircuts and untidy turbans balanced precariously on their heads. Suddenly, an elderly Sikh walked up to him, clutched his hands and cried inconsolably. The old man's hair was bunched up in a small bun and he released Chhatwal's hands only to fold his own in reverence. He spoke a single sentence but repeated it twice in chaste Punjabi: 'Please give me a turban? I want nothing else.' Chattwal despaired at the unusual request and told me how that one sentence had transformed him from an Indian Air Force officer preparing for post-retirement life to a committed volunteer.

The ageing Sikh's demand for a turban underscored a much deeper aspect of the 1984 riots: the issue of a lost identity and the struggle to either regain or discard it completely. But why did a piece of unstitched garment, merely five yards long, become symbolic of a community's self-esteem? Why was it that more than two decades later, the community still viewed the loss of headgear as a terrible affront?

Legend has it that the turban was made an integral part of Sikhism in 1699 by the last or the tenth guru, Gobind Singh. He is also credited with the concept of *chardi kala* (the rising spirit); *sawa lakh se ik ladaon* (one single Sikh fighting a hundred and twenty-five thousand people—suggestive of unyielding courage in the face of impossible odds) and laid out a path to realise Guru Nanak's objectives in which the creation of the Khalsa Panth or Order was integral. Khalsa or a "pure" Sikh was deemed as one who carried and exhibited on his person the five articles of faith or the 5 *ks*: *kesh, kara, kanga, kachcha* and *kirpan* (unshorn hair and beard, steel bracelet, wooden comb, drawers or underpants and sword). Therefore, the turban was not an "adornment" which could be replaced by a cap or by keeping the hair matted. It was first adopted as a necessity and gradually converted into a symbol of faith. The orthodoxy amongst Sikhism often argue that by tying a turban, a Sikh affirms his commitment to the principles of justice and equality and that he or she assumes the role of an ambassador of faith.

However, during the pre-insurgency period in Punjab, the turban was by and large a personal choice and not necessarily an assertion of one's religiosity. Yet, even amongst non-believers, the turban represented a freedom of choice and the attempts to forcibly take it away, a violation of human rights. It is only when Sikhs began to be viewed with suspicion that significant groups within the community moved closer to the more strident aspect of the faith preached by Guru Gobind Singh than the benign and anti-ritual teachings of Guru Nanak Dev. And with the outward signs of the Khalsa Order and most importantly, the turban ascribing a self-image to Sikhs' cultural-religiosity, the headgear became mandatory.

For instance, on the morning of 1 November, veteran journalist Sunil Sethi's query (at fellow-scribe Coomi Kapoor's home) was "normal", when viewed against this backdrop. He saw her Sikh neighbours and instantly shot out: 'Where has your turban gone? Why are you guys wearing cricket caps?' Sethi narrated this incident while moderating a discussion on the anti-Sikh carnage in Delhi in February 2014. Both the father and son had taken off their turbans (the young boy anyway wore a *patka*), rolled up their hair on top of their heads, and rested cricket caps over it. While Delhi was burning, Sunil found himself making a query that was clearly tragicomic. Tragic because Sunil thought of making a similar suggestion to his Sikh neighbours who had taken refuge in his house. Comic because in a city where smoke was rising from all directions, Sunil found himself asking a ludicrous question: 'Where can I get these cricket caps?' At the panel discussion, Sunil mentioned the incident to emphasise that for most non-Sikhs like him, the loss of hair and turban was the first ominous sign.

As mentioned above, prior to the separatist movement in Punjab, Sikh identity was not necessarily centered either around the turban or the *kirpan*. In the Punjab of yore, it was fairly common for Punjabi Hindu families to pledge their eldest male child as a *keshdhari* (bearer of long hair), while other male members of the same family wore their hair short.

Traditionally speaking, there were three distinct categories amongst Sikhs: *amritdhari* (the pristine one who underwent the *amrit*-imbibing ritual—a form of baptism); *keshdhari* and *sahajdhari* (born into Sikh families but sans an overt Sikh identity). Before the insurgency in Punjab began dominating public debate in north India, Sikhs could opt for any variant, but still be regarded as part of the community. But beginning with the early Eighties, *sahajdhari* Sikhs were no longer considered members of the community and the lines between *amritdharis* and *keshdharis* gradually blurred. As one of the dominant signatures of the 1984 carnage was to deny surviving male Sikhs recognition, many accepted the diktat and over time slowly obliterated their identities while others fought on. The struggle for retaining or moving on from a socially acceptable identity as a Sardar continued and was yet to be resolved. Some, like Sunil Sethi and Coomi Kapoor's friends opted for a tactical alteration in their looks which enabled them to be passed off as non-Sikhs and once the situation went back to normalcy, they returned to their previous identities. Among those whose hair was either forcibly cut or those who clipped them of their own accord, significant numbers "went back" to looking like Sikhs, while others remained faithfuls but were nervous of returning to their previous avatars. Even among those who did not alter their identity during 1984, many eventually succumbed to pressure from the constant gawking and extra-scrutiny from security forces.

From the beginning of 1984, especially after Operation Blue Star, a "reverse discovery" of identity also surfaced amongst the Sikhs. Several who in a sense "returned home", donned the outward Sikh identity not because they sympathised with Sikh separatists but out of a sense of outrage against the government's decision to send in troops into the Golden Temple and of being labelled as traitors by the State. For the orthodoxy, such "homecoming" was welcome but in the 1990s after reports of a sharp decline in *amritdhari* and *keshdhari* Sikhs, there were concerted efforts at the community level and local gurudwaras to restore the religious identity of Sikhs. Rama Lakshmi in the *Washington Post* examined the rising trend of cutting hair amongst Sikhs in Punjab, as follows:

> Although there are no formal surveys, community groups say that only 25 percent of Sikhs younger than 30 follow the practice. Many young Sikhs say the daily tedium of combing and tying up their long hair and a desire to assimilate are pushing them to give up the turban...

On the other hand, there were also a few courses in "turban-tying", particularly for the young. In April 2005, a self-styled group called, Akal Purakh Ki Fauj or the Army of the Timeless

Being, organised an annual Turban Pride Day. It sent volunteers to teach turban-tying in schools, introduced a software program called Smart Turban to help people pick a style that suited them besides organising Kaumi Dastaarbandi Smaagam encouraging children to tie *dastaars* or short turbans (also worn by Sikh women). Other groups established motivational camps where special sessions were held periodically.

But the issue remains unresolved partly because of dissent amongst various groups over what constitutes Sikhism and Sikh identity. Several contend that in order to be a true Sikh, one must undergo baptism and lead a regulated life, with abstinence as the cornerstone. Then there are others who believe that a true Sikh is someone who keeps his hair unshorn. Still others hold the view that following the *gurbani* or the word of god is sufficient. It is consequently evident that the turban is not essential in the construction of the Sikh identity. But this perception gets altered in the view of not just non-Sikhs but also official bodies like the Shiromani Gurudwara Prabandhak Committee or SGPC which grants exclusive voting rights for elections to its management committee to *amritdhari* and *keshdhari* Sikhs despite a strong sentiment in favour of the *sehajdharis*. The principal institutions of Sikhism lay overt emphasis on orthodoxy—which in the recent past came to be put on even keel with Sikh separatism. As in the case of most religious minorities the world over, being devout is often also interpreted as political radicalism. As a result, Sikh identity in the personal realm has failed to come into its own and remains cloistered in a narrow view of what defines a male Sikh. A five-yard-long fabric has willy-nilly become the sole identity of Sikhs and only because of the manner in which it was treated in 1984.

After bearing the burden of his identity for more than two years, Arvind Bedi walked into a hair cutting salon one winter afternoon accompanied by a friend and his brother-in-law, a former Indian

Air Force officer. The barber at the fancy Delhi's Defence Services Officers' Institute couldn't believe his ears when he heard Arvind's brother-in-law say: '*Sahab ke baal utaar do*' (Give him a haircut).

After a while, the man with a new identity exited the salon. The black turban he had worn for years was neatly folded and tucked under his arm. He later shoved it inside the tool box of his scooter and went to office where he worked in the security department. At the gate, the guard who had been Arvind's junior for close to a decade walked up to inform the unfamiliar visitor that it was a second Saturday and the office was shut for public dealing. This was Arvind's first introduction to his new self.

Arvind then headed towards his wife's office. Tears trickled down her eyes as they made their way to the day-care centre to pick up their six-month-old daughter who recoiled at a stranger holding out his arms towards her. It was only when Arvind called her name softly that the baby smiled and yelped with joy.

Years later, she would look at the pictures of the handsome, turbaned Sikh and empathise when he cried each time while watching *Maachis* (the Hindi film directed by the renowned filmmaker, Gulzar in 1996) and particularly the scene in which a young man explains the reasons for cutting his hair. The young girl understood when her father spoke about the shame—how he had scampered away like a mouse.

However unlike the young man in *Maachis,* Arvind's reason for altering his identity was triggered by a stone that did not quite travel on the morning of 1 November 1984. Had it landed on cue, he wouldn't have been spared. As a key member of the security set-up for a significant part of south Delhi's power supply, 31 October had been a hectic day for Arvind. Despite the news of the assassination, he went about inspecting the vulnerable sites, and it was only in the evening, after being forewarned about the violence on Delhi's streets that he had decided to stay at a friend's house in Ramakrishna Puram.

Early next morning, Arvind decided to take stock of the situation and went for a stroll to a nearby market. The place was abuzz with everyday activity but just when Arvind was making his way back to his friend's home, he saw a group of people staring intently at him. Arvind quickened his steps and went back to pick up his scooter.

It happened when he was waiting for the lights to change at the traffic intersection in Munirka, a short distance away from his friend's home. He first noticed a mob walking towards him followed by a roar from a group of youngsters who were watching him from the street corner. Arvind let out a blood-curdling scream when he saw an arm go up to hurl a stone at him. The young man retreated and Arvind zipped off on his scooter.

Fortunately, the by-lanes of Munirka was familiar terrain and Arvind soon reached home. The next few days passed in a blur during which his family was shifted by friends to a "safe home" of a professor at the Indian Institute of Technology.

Soon Arvind returned to work, as did his wife and others in the family. But something had changed drastically. Arvind developed a fear of the crowds and would feel his limbs go numb whenever he was accosted by people. He and his wife even moved home in preparation for the arrival of a child but Arvind could never overcome the feeling of being "spotted". His sense of panic was also magnified by the fact that the Sikh who had driven him to various installations on 31 October had gone missing (it later turned out that on 1 November, a mob had barged into his house and burnt him alive). At every public place, Arvind sensed an extra once-over, a stricter scrutiny from men manning the gates. He was slowly convinced that the reason was his turban.

At a personal level however, Arvind had a precedent in his own family. Days before the verdict of the 1984 election, which handed Rajiv Gandhi the biggest electoral mandate in Indian political history, his eldest brother had returned home from office sans his turban.

Eventually in December 1986, after agonising over the matter for two long years during which he was frequently haunted by scenes of people chasing and attacking him, Arvind decided to opt for the irreversible alteration.

On 7 January 1987, Arvind made it to the pages of *The Statesman* but his identity remained hidden behind a fictitious name, Hemendra Singh. The newspaper article began with a basic account: how he had a "hair-cut for the first time in his life a few days ago because he no longer felt safe on the roads of Delhi". And further added:

> With this act, Hemendra Singh has joined a number of Sikhs outside Punjab who have been taking this "vital" step over the past two years. A common bond between them is a fear psychosis which has gripped them following the riots in November 1984. And average people that they were, who knew all too well that their personal well-being was linked to their city of domicile and not to a fantasy called Khalistan, they gradually took the "painful step". It was painful because in spite of the fact that the turban and the beard "had no religious meaning" for them, but were purely a "question of physical identity of an individual". Hemendra Singh also joins a number of Hindus in Punjab who have also taken a similar decision though of the opposite nature. Hounded by terrorists and unwilling to forsake the land of their forefathers, they have decided to stay on with a new identity. The person remains the same, except that the till now clean shaven cheeks are plastered with uninterrupted beard and the head sports a saffron turban.

Hemendra Singh was a name this author gave to his friend, and whose approval I hadn't sought before writing the article. I remember how he kept talking about the guilt. The act of cutting his hair weighed on his conscience, he said. But does he feel the same in 2014? I asked him. 'No. Much has changed in India since then... I realised that I hadn't betrayed anyone by deciding to shun the turban. Rather, *my* India failed me.'

In the deep recess of one of her cupboards, his wife carefully retained the long strips of black cloth that Arvind tied around his head. The couple's decision to cling on to a symbol—a virtual personal artefact—of a time that was more perfect, reflected a deep pain and anguish.

Strangely his new identity impacted his religiosity in more ways than one. For several years after cutting his hair, Arvind avoided going to a gurudwara but when he began revisiting the shrines later, each episode would trigger an emotional purge and he would seek atonement for his sins. It was obvious he desired acceptance but felt it was somehow unattainable.

So far as Arvind's daughter, Minnie or Shibani was concerned, the missing turban was an integral part of her childhood. By the time she was four or five, she knew the turban was absent in her home while it sat prominently on the heads of her grandfathers and several other male members in the family. Although there was never an exclusive session to "explain" the reason for her father's cropped hair, every electoral victory by the Congress party would strangely trigger murmurs within the family. By the time she turned fourteen, Shibani knew her family's connection with 1984.

Shibani is now in her mid-Twenties and represents a generation whose parents were victimised in 1984 and hope for justice during every election. When I spoke to her in 2014, it came as no surprise that she was bitterly opposed to the Congress party. 'But not only for its mishandling of 1984,' she was quick to add. By a quirk or coincidence, Shibani's political viewpoint was firmed up when public resentment against the Congress party-led coalition was beginning to coalesce around 2011. As a TV professional, she recalled how excited she would be to produce news bulletins in support of the movement. But soon the euphoria evaporated and the futility of agitations became a system of belief for her.

It is interesting how her generation swings between two extremes—one represented by Harmeet Kaur who goes out to protest because it is important to keep pressing for a closure.

Whereas Shibani wants the guilty punished but does not consider public protests as practical interventions. One is vehemently desirous of only marrying a Sikh, the other wastes no time over such issues. Drawn from virtually the same demographic group, it is fascinating how the young women present a challenge and opportunity to political groups. It is up to them to cultivate or disregard the Harmeets and Shibanis of Delhi, as they have routinely done since 1984.

One day in 1997 when Hartej or Teji (the latter was more cool and hence preferable) was four years old, he returned from school and told his mother that he wanted to be a *boy* and not a Sardar. Some years later, in an upmarket Mumbai school, he resented when some of his classmates commented that boys like him (who had long hair and tied it up as a knot on top of their heads), were either stupid or good athletes! He was neither. As a musician, he performed gigs with metal bands and joined in frenzied rounds of headbanging inside mosh pits.

But Teji's hair grew incredibly long and he soon acquired a reputation for his thick mane. Once, by which time it had snaked past his knees, even Bollywood actor Salman Khan commented about it! But none of this neutralised Teji's discomfort about looking "different"—he was never included in the school choir or given parts in plays because he was a Sikh. Finally, when he turned fourteen, Teji mustered up the courage and told his father that he wanted to cut his hair.

His father had also got used to an acronym for a name: K J. That's how the professional world knows K J Singh—the acclaimed sound engineer in the Indian music industry whom we encountered earlier in this book. In fact the name is a short form of the official version: Kanwarjit Singh Sawhney and the result of a recalcitrant graphic artist in Doordarshan who found his name far too lengthy while typing the end credits-roll for a TV show!

The first time his son expressed a desire to cut his hair, K J was shell-shocked. He bought time by asking the young chap to hold on till he turned eighteen. Teji agreed but after his tenth standard board exams finally presented his parents with an ultimatum.

It may be recalled that as a youngster, K J Singh was hardly aware of his religious identity. One day when he was in the college canteen with his girlfriend Poonam (later his wife), the two saw an advertisement posted by the now-defunct HMV for the job of an Artists and Repertoire Manager. Among other specifications, it mentioned that the applicant must have a reasonable knowledge of English, Hindi and Punjabi. K J paused over this last condition to ponder if he met the requirement when his eyes suddenly fell on his own shadow cast by the afternoon light. He then turned to Poonam and said in no uncertain terms that he would refuse to let anyone know about his fluency in Punjabi only because it was an assumption in his case! After all, for K J, religious identity was inconsequential and despite the sudden revelation in the shadow of a turbaned gent.

However all that changed in the Eighties when turbaned heads and bearded faces were singled out in crowds and by 1983 became akin to a wrong flag on one's head. As Sikh terrorists routinely pulled out Hindus from buses, the effort of maintaining one's identity became extremely tenuous even for people like K J Singh. In his case the problem was further accentuated because although his family was deeply religious—especially his mother—none of them were overtly ritualistic. Therefore, K J was wedded to his physical appearance more out of habit and less due to adherence. At no point did K J want to cut his hair nor wish to enforce his belief on others who opted to do so either before or after 1984. For instance, after joining the music industry, K J began wearing a trademark wraparound turban only because the traditional headgear interfered in his profession as a sound engineer.

I asked K J about Punjab and he said, 'The more serious act of desecration was the initial decision to turn a blind eye to terrorists taking control and not the eventual action to rid the shrine of gun-totting marauders. But the anti-Sikh riots devastated me completely...'

I also learnt that K J's admission to a Canadian university was delayed because of the riots and he eventually made it in the fall of 1985 and found himself in the midst of a volatile Sikh community. He recalled how his indoctrination had begun with a slide show procured surreptitiously by a reputed lawyer. But it came to naught as K J found the collective chest-beating unbearable.

As Teji's deadline came closer, these contradictions resurfaced in K J's mind. He confessed to Poonam that just as he had decided to retain the identity of a Sikh, he wanted his son to follow suit.

Teji approached his father yet again and K J told his son that he would agree, provided the boy sought his grandfather's permission. But the tactic failed. When the boy demurred at the idea of speaking directly to the ageing patriarch, K J spoke to his father and told him that his grandson had a peculiar request to make. The old man heard him out and  acquiesced!

It was obvious that Teji, much like his famous father, couldn't be governed by custom and family convention. He believed that social identities based on caste, creed and religion were transitory and often argued how Greece had survived despite the disappearance of an entire Pantheon of Gods! Still the "event" assumed dramatic proportions. To begin with, the family did not know where to take him for a haircut and how the boy was to shave on a regular basis! Eventually guided by some associates in the film industry, Teji was taken to a nearby outlet of Hakim Alim's chain of salons. The appointed day began with the mother and son visiting the gurudwara and then heading to the salon.

As expected, Teji was ecstatic with relief while K J preserved his son's hair in a small bag as a keepsake.

❈ ❈ ❈ ❈

Unlike K J, Joginder Singh did no such thing. He recoiled at the ugly stumps of hair on his sons' heads. It was 3 November and he was being evacuated with his family in an Army truck to Farash Bazar. Although he was a Sikligar Sikh, the forty-five-year-old ironsmith preferred death over cutting his hair. His sons, Balbir and Jasbir were not as resolute. As mentioned in chapter two of this book, it was their hair that had flown through the room and made the dough unpalatable, leaving all of them hungry for three days.

Ten days after the riots, the family returned to find their home destroyed; even the cheap electric bulbs were smashed to smithereens. It was obvious that the issue of identity was inconsequential for Joginder.

In time, Balbir moved to Haridwar with his family and Jasbir got married to Harjinder Kaur. The young bride never found it odd that the man she was engaged to was a Sikh but wasn't when she married him! A son was born to them in 1987 and in deference to Joginder and Surjit Kaur, the little boy called Ranjit was raised as a Sikh. But even he faced derision in class and one day, the six year old convinced his grandparents that he wanted to wear his hair like the rest of his classmates. Surjit Kaur wept to see her eldest grandson discard the turban but the little fellow was relieved and in no time forgot about his Sikh identity.

A few years later, the owners of Block 32, Trilokpuri, where Joginder and his family once lived, sold off their homes and found willing buyers amongst Muslims who were far removed from the carnage of 1984. Over time, the *Ik Omkar* sign was replaced with the star and crescent and green flags dotted the skyline.

❈ ❈ ❈ ❈

For Prof J P S Uberoi, November 1984 didn't come as a surprise. A familiar, black-turbaned figure in the prestigious Delhi School of Economics, the self-effacing teacher had felt it in his bones since Operation Blue Star. It felt familiar like 1947 and the Partition when as a twelve year old, he had lived in transit refugee camps.

A decade later, it was on a ship bound for England that the Professor approached the barber and severed the final link with his Sikh identity. Over time, he became, what his daughter Safina described as "a goatee-sporting liberal and atheist". In 1969, propelled by a surge of patriotism following the 1965 Indo-Pak war and with another one looming ahead, Uberoi returned to India with an Australian wife.

It may be recalled that on the fifth day of the customary ten-day-long Akhand Path held in memory of the Professor's father, the Centre had launched Operation Blue Star and a curfew was imposed in the state of Punjab. At the end of the funeral ceremony, Prof Uberoi was asked to follow the ritual of tying a turban, signifying the assumption of familial responsibilities as the head and next of kin. The seventeen-year-old Safina watched her father go through the ritual and was struck by the realisation that he was *becoming* a Sikh once again. This was like a homecoming of sorts and unlike on board the ship to England when he had broken a taboo, this time he was accepting it willingly.

Soon the Uberois returned to Delhi and the first thing that disturbed both Patricia and Safina was the black turban on the Professor's head! It was almost like an open invitation for Sikh-baiters and something the family dreaded post the patriarch's death. Later it came as no surprise when Safina's brother, Prem enlisted in the Australian army and served a four-year term before finally quitting. The decision had to do with an unnerving experience during his grandfather's funeral ceremony. One day during a short curfew break, Prem had stepped out to fetch a bucket of water from one of the municipal taps and in his enthusiasm to reach before others, had sprinted wildly—an act that did not meet the approval of a few policemen stationed on top of armoured trucks that patrolled the streets of Chandigarh. More than two decades later, Prem recounted how people of Indian origin in Australia would ask him if he loved India? Prem was honest and said: 'It is very hard to love a country that had tried to kill you.'

Prem's claim wasn't exaggerated as his family had to flee their home like fugitives in the aftermath of Indira Gandhi's assassination. The Professor had sneaked out of his home through the back door which opened into a narrow alleyway used by sweepers to empty garbage. Among other precious personal objects, J P S Uberoi left his turban behind but remembered to pick up a photograph of Jarnail Singh Bhindranwale  which he tore and flung over  rubbish heaps. Finally, after bumbling past heaps of rubbish, the ageing don reached a friend's house where his family was locked up for several days.

The story of 1984 was severely impacted by both the assertion and annihilation of identities. Swaranpreet Singh, the doctor we met in the previous chapters was a  disillusioned man when he left India in 1991. Prior to his departure, although he had struggled with his identity and questioned the relevance of the Khalsa Order, not once did he consider cutting his hair in England. And finally, when he did, it had nothing to do with 1984 and in no way altered his perspective on the carnage.

As a professional psychiatrist treating post-traumatic stress, Swaranpreet often delved deep into what led people to make choices. Despite undergoing similar experiences, why had Sikhs reacted differently to 1984? For instance, K J Singh chose not to cut his hair but Arvind did. Why did Joginder refuse to cut his hair but raised no objections when his sons trimmed their locks in his presence? How was it that Safina became a "Sikh child" after 1984 while her two siblings drifted far from their father's religion? After failing to find peace, Swaranpreet left India while K J came back to make peace with his country. One retained his identity as a Sikh while the other opted to forsake it almost a decade and a half later. Yet, they remained bound by the search for an identity which was catalysed by the violence of 1984.

# Seven

# Postcards from Bokaro

Paramjit Kaur stared fixedly at the chappati on her plate and then looked around the dimly-lit room to exchange glances with her three siblings. Two women in their mid-Twenties, teachers at a local school, cajoled the four softly; one advised the kids to dip the chappati in the glass of milk they had been served because there was no *sabzi* or vegetable. The other explained that they must eat to survive the ordeal. For the first time in her life, the fifteen-year-old Paramjit realised how painful eating could be and remembered it forever.

The previous evening, news had filtered into Dugdha, a small industrial township, which was a short distance away from Bokaro (in today's Jharkhand), and best known for a coal washery unit. Indira Gandhi had been assassinated. Strangely, the town didn't come to a screeching halt and sensing no obvious danger, Paramjit's father had gone about his domestic chores after returning from work. That evening it included carrying a sack of wheat to the neighbourhood *atta chakki* (flour mill) shop. Suddenly someone from the crowd, perhaps a customer or a hanger-on, asked

Paramjit's father if the flour was to make *ladoos* to celebrate Indira Gandhi's assassination? Word got around and within hours, the silly joke turned on them and mobs began advancing towards the homes of twenty-five Sikh families in Dugdha.

Inside the house, Paramjit's parents were terrified and clutched the children to their bosoms. Suddenly, there was a loud banging on the back door and they fled to another room and locked themselves in. The noise abated but there was a fresh worry—something was burning. It was the back door which had been bathed in kerosene and torched before the mob purposefully headed in another direction. The four children assisted in dousing the flames and the family spent the night praying. The next morning as word got around, the teachers arrived and escorted the children to their home. The parents remained inside—this time a lock hung outside the door to ward off the killers.

After a few days, Dugdha returned to normalcy and Paramjit went back to school, but she faced hatred from friends; taunts and barbs became routine and the children openly accused her of being a co-conspirator in Indira Gandhi's assassination. The more she argued, the greater was the shame. But the young girl was undeterred and made a solemn pledge: one day she will go to college and only to escape the humiliation forever....

A few years later, Paramjit redeemed her promise and secured admission to the Rajendra Institute of Medical Sciences in Ranchi and met Sushil Kumar, who was from Bihar and two years her senior. In time both graduated, married and had two children. The family of four was an interesting mix—the children were encouraged to follow both religions and given the option to make a choice. Over time, the 1984 trauma was partially exorcised or so Paramjit thought...

When I first met Paramjit, her voice cracked several times while recalling those days and nights of November 1984. During the interview, Sushil would often look at her endearingly as if to push back the surge of anguish which threatened to make its way at different points.

'Initially, I often wondered if something had gone wrong inside my head?' said she. After Paramjit earned her spurs as a medic, she was convinced  it wasn't a medical condition and eventually overcame a cusp in her mind. She concluded her interview by saying that if the night of 31 October 1984 were to recur, there would be no question of a cowering response. Instead it would be one based on the Hammurabi's Code.

I boarded the train to Dhanbad en route Bokaro wondering if I had become a purveyor of tragedies; on a mission to probe those who had made peace with the past? Paramjit had already proved me wrong.

Sixty-year-old Iqbal Singh, resident of Gomoh, a small town in the district of Dhanbad was thirty years old in 1984. On 31 October, he was  in Punjab on a business tour with his friends and decided to have a meal at the *langar* or community kitchen in the Golden Temple. After the news, the group  abandoned their original plan to return home. Instead they first boarded a train to Ludhiana and after assurances from several quarters, decided to head for Dhanbad the next night.

The train hurtled along peaceably at night but by the next morning, frenzied mobs were sighted at platforms. Iqbal Singh and his friends cowered under the seats with turbans in their hands and hid from gangs who trooped through compartments. Occasionally a loud cry followed by ululation would rent the air: "We got a Sardar!" As the train pulled out of a station, a murderous crowd was seen converging around a hapless Sikh.

By the time the train reached Lucknow, there were scores who patrolled the train station looking for Sikhs crouching inside compartments. Finally, Iqbal's luck ran out and he was pulled out of the train along with a friend. The crowd first emptied their pockets of all the cash and valuables, and then beat them severely. Even as Iqbal bent over to protect his abdomen from injuries, the faces around him started to blur and he felt faint.

The train blew a long whistle and the two were carried away by some people. Over the next few days, a Juvenile Remand Home in Lucknow became the temporary abode for almost five hundred Sikhs necessitating the then chief minister of UP, N D Tiwari to make a visit to the *relief camp.*

Meanwhile back home in Dhanbad, Iqbal Singh's mother would sit from dawn to dusk at the Gomoh railway station awaiting her son's arrival. The same scene would play out every evening before someone would cajole her to go home and rest before returning the next morning. Eventually, arrangements were made for the inmates' journey; tickets were bought and a small posse of policemen escorted the group of Sikhs to their destinations.

After what had seemed impossible a few days ago, the train reached Gomoh as scheduled and the moment news spread of Iqbal's arrival, large crowds thronged the station. Iqbal's mother broke down on seeing her son and so did his pregnant wife who gave birth to a baby girl two days later. The little girl grew up listening to her father's incredible story and when Iqbal bid her farewell after her wedding in April 2013, he extracted a promise from his son-in-law to never forget.

My journey took me to Dhanbad, the coal city best known for twin infamies: *Gangs of Wasseypur,* the film based on criminals who roam the bylanes driving terror into people and the treacherous mines with men crawling in its underbelly for a livelihood. I used the city as a base to go to Bokaro which was once in united Bihar, but was later hived off as part of Jharkhand in November 2000.

The first thing that struck me was how the Misra Commission had begun probing the violence in the city almost a year after the riots, in September 1985. This was obviously a result of an ill-disposed government led by Rajiv Gandhi which constituted the Misra Commission belatedly in April 1985* (see pages 133-34). Unfortunately the panel was not even mandated to probe the violence on trains and Bokaro along with Dhanbad and Haryana had reported a large number of such casualties. Despite the contentious conclusions vis-a-vis the carnage in Delhi, the Misra Commission gave an insightful overview of the violence in Bokaro:

> There is no dispute about the number of deaths in Bokaro and Chas Tehsils. The actual riot at these places took place on November 1, 1984, after imposition of curfew in the morning. Total deaths are admitted to be of 69 Sikhs (this number was revised to 78 in subsequent years)—on account of police firing on riotous mobs three non-Sikhs also died. The situation in these two Tehsils was brought under effective control and normalised by the afternoon of November 1. A good number of people were killed in Dashmesh Nagar area where an unauthorised Gurudwara and a small colony of Sikhs were razed to the ground and everyone of that community found during the riot was done to death.

The Commission also pointed towards police apathy and this despite the fact that Bokaro was the only city where the police had opened fire on rioters.

Prior to Bokaro, Dhanbad was my first halt in the region dominated by coal and steel cities to understand how people had coped. At some point, my sense of despair had begun to insulate me from the real purpose of the book and particularly when I discovered how Dhanbad had been eclipsed from the map of the carnage. If at all there were any references, it was because Bokaro was still a part of Dhanbad district before it became a separate administrative unit in 1991. The coal city's negligible connection with 1984 underscored a painful fact reiterated earlier in this book: there was little or no documentation available of the violence; neither official nor any other efforts were made to maintain any records. That night as the train inched through a cloud of thick fog, I hoped to find someone who remembered.

❊ ❊ ❊ ❊

Earlier in the morning, an email exchange heralded an unlikely entrant into the story. Vishy Kuruganti, whose Twitter handle described him as: "Entrepreneur. Barefoot runner. Vegan experimenter. Reva owner. Minimalist."

Vishy lived in Bengaluru and after holding several technology leadership positions in the United States, had returned to India in August 2008 to "chase his dreams". One of these was mGaadi, a social enterprise that functioned as a technology-driven interface between auto-drivers and customers in the city. However on 10 March 2010, he did something extraordinarily different by using the "Send All" option on his school alumni group.

Vishy spent his early childhood in Bokaro and left in 1983 after his father was transferred to Vishakhapatnam Steel Plant in Andhra Pradesh. In college, he kept in touch with his school friends sporadically but after technology became the great enabler, his old gang reconnected and even organised a reunion in Dallas in 2006. It was on one such occasion after the *pappi-jhappi* (hugging and back-slapping, to put it loosely) and the standard catch-catch with *where have you been* queries had been exhausted, that the "other" things resurfaced. Stories about how "all the Sikh families had sought refuge in the school...the Army tanks...Sikh boys and men cutting their hair... how one of their close friend's home was attacked" etc. Vishy left the reunion party with a sense of disquiet. The evening had brought back dark memories of 1984. Vishy articulated his sense of outrage to me in an email:

> To my sister and me (and possibly thousands of Bokaro kids), it was a Stephen King's *It* moment (a peaceful Derry shattered by an ugliness and brutality we couldn't imagine was present in our idyllic town).

Besides reigniting memories, the school reunion also spurred Vishy to document the experiences of a shared episode. But most importantly, there was one question that had bothered him since the Dallas party in 2006: before 1984, had he and his friends ignored the latent biases in Bokaro? Somehow this kept replaying in my head and even I was forced to think—why had Bokaro erupted in such a frenzy when it had had no past history of communal tension or violence?

I found no definite answers but a few interesting analyses enabled me to arrive at an inference. In the aftermath of Operation Blue Star in June 1984, Sikh soldiers had mutinied in three different army cantonments across India, of which in one of the most violent episodes in Ramgarh (located between Bokaro and Ranchi), the Sikh Regimental Centre's Commanding Officer, Brigadier Gen R S Puri was killed brutally. The intensity of violence against Sikhs in parts of south Bihar was mainly a result of this so-called "betrayal", and also due to its proximity to Ramgarh cantonment and the main railway line which regularly ferried Sikh soldiers. However, I felt that we were skimming the surface and decided to probe further and went back a couple of years.

The Bokaro Steel Plant was established in the mid-1960s as part of a collaborative project with the erstwhile Soviet Union. In 1972 after the first blast furnace became functional, the township grew in fits and starts and by 2011 transformed into a city with a population of 5.63 lakhs. Reminiscent of several industrial townships set up during the post-Nehruvian era, the Steel City attracted skilled workforce from various parts of the country who later assimilated into exclusive groups or clubs. Gradually, Bokaro also had several cultural associations which were formed on the basis of sub-national identities like, the Telugu Samajam, Kairali, Bangiya Samaj and so on. Everyday when Bokaro's children opened their tiffin boxes in schools, they unpacked pieces of India's culinary mosaic evoking a stereotypical DAVP advertisement for the country's diversity!

Meanwhile the Sikhs in the city, despite their insignificant numerical presence, were respected as an industrious community primarily because after Partition, a large number of migrants had initiated new business ventures in eastern India and gradually became influential members of Bokaro society. This was severely resented by the locals and when the riots broke out in November 1984, the Sikhs were targeted en masse irrespective of their economic status. According to the 1981 census, the Sikhs accounted for a meagre 0.11 per cent of the total population in united Bihar. Later in 2001—the first census undertaken after the formation of Jharkhand—the district of Bokaro had a population of 0.32 per cent or a total of 5,631 Sikhs. In Dhanbad, the percentage was a shade higher at 0.51, accounting for a total population of 12,140. Although there are no exact figures available, there is evidence of Sikhs migrating in large numbers to Punjab after the 1984 carnage. For instance, several relatives of Kulbir Singh (see chapter Three, The Horror! The Horror!), had relocated to different parts of Punjab.

Their tragedies were similar to forty-three-year-old Gurdip Singh's who was a joint owner in a family-run spare parts shop in Morabadi, Ranchi. His father retired as Captain from the Indian Army and had settled in Ranchi. A few days after the riots, Gurdip Singh demanded a division in the family property and less than a fortnight later, on 13 November 1984, he moved to Amritsar with his wife and children.

In the next three decades, Gurdip tried his hand at several jobs in Amritsar but had failed each time. Later three of Gurdip's brothers also followed him to Punjab and set up mediocre businesses in Ludhiana while the other two chose to stay back in Jharkhand.

Why had Gurdip fled in desperation? What had become so unbearable in a city that had seen him through his childhood? The answer was quite simply this: despite the obvious hatred and violence in 1984, the one thing that Gurdip had failed to accept was the culpability of his neighbours during the rampage.

However Kulbir or Gurdip's relatives were not the only ones to have moved away from the region after the events of 1984. During the course of my interactions in Dhanbad and other cities and towns of Jharkhand, I came across several instances of Sikhs migrating to Punjab primarily in search of safety. An estimate published by the *Tehelka* magazine in December 2007 mentioned that of the '8,000 Sikh families living in these areas in 1984, only about 2,500 remain.'

For instance, Jasbinder Grewal who grew up in Bokaro before joining college in Chandigarh. In October 1984, she understood what it meant to have Hell descend on one's doorstep. Yet, she had chosen to remain quiet until Vishy's mail landed in her inbox in March 2010. It took her just eight hours to respond:

> We felt lucky and very-very blessed to be alive…as some of our family friends were either killed or had lost a child. We came back to an empty home…I only cried because I had lost most of my school pics and memories…My mom started having nightmares and by the end of November my mom, brother and sister accompanied me to Chandigarh—never to return to Bokaro. Dad continued with his job thinking he could take a transfer but that somehow did not happen. So for the next 15 years he visited us twice a year in Chandigarh. My brother and sis(ter) joined St Xaviers School, Chandigarh but believe me it wasn't anywhere close to our school. Life was ok except we were living in those times when terrorism was at its peak in Punjab. So curfew being clamped on the city was a way of life. There was no life after 6:00 p.m. Nobody ventured outdoors after 6:00 p.m., and if you did, you did not return.

I tracked Jasbinder down to Chicago where she lives with her husband and two children, aged fourteen and eleven. Over several email exchanges, I also discovered that although Jasbinder's mother had been severely impacted by the tragedy, she glossed over her own loss and lamented the fate of others who had battled grave injustices. Jasbinder recalled how at an impromptu shelter camp in her school, her mother would be inconsolable about a family which lived on the top floor of a four-storied house and was pushed out and even as each one lay dying on the floor, the mob had doused them with kerosene and lit a pyre. Or the insurance agent who grieved for his daughter who was raped and killed or the ordeal of three young girls who had escaped from their home through the bathroom window while the mobs bashed their parents to death with iron rods in the living room.

Jasbinder wrote to me:

> These incidents just broke my mom and I saw her change in the camp. She went about comforting the families during the day but would cry uncontrollably in the night. We came home after 10 days of living in the camp and in a week we boarded the train to Chandigarh, never to return… She is now scared of everyone…does not trust anyone beside her immediate family. She still wakes up in the middle of the night to check on doors and windows. She has nightmares where she screams and wakes up the entire home. She hates bringing up the subject of 1984 riots…because it brings back memories of tragedies in the life of people who were our extended families…

And then there was Priti Haneja, whose idyllic life in the quaint little town was shattered in an instant. The moment Priti's father had heard of mobs patrolling the streets, he had taken refuge at a nearby police station but left his daughter in the care of his non-Sikh neighbour who was also his colleague. The man of the house was travelling and his family resented Priti's presence and the little girl was instructed to stay holed up in a room. She would periodically strain her ears and overhear people speaking in whispers. Sometimes even a grim warning that was issued to the family: '*Bhabhi* (elder brother's wife)… by allowing this girl to stay in your house, you are putting yourself at risk….Get her out!'

Even though many in her family were Punjabi Hindus, Priti grew up resenting every non-Sikh; her community was suddenly under suspicion while she had grown up on stories of their valour. She wrote to me:

> Almost every other day I have been sitting in front of my writing … sometimes some words came and many times they didn't.

Priti's faith was somewhat restored but only after Sunil Singh's account was added to "Bokaro Tales" by Vishy Kuruganti.

The morning after Indira Gandhi's assassination, Sunil's father was lounging in his home in a dhoti-vest and chatting with a friend who had dropped by. The two were worried about the ominous signs visible in the columns of rising smoke from the direction of a neighbouring village cluster called Chas. Sunil was helping his mother set the lunch table while his younger brother, Sujit was somewhere in the neighbourhood. Shortly after 1:00 pm, the young boy came running in and exclaimed, 'Sardar uncle's house is being attacked!' Everybody peered out of the window and saw that their neighbour, Gill's car was set on fire. Sunil's father immediately strode out with his young son, and the rest was described by Sunil as follows:

> I followed my dad scared about his life and thinking I have the strength to save him. Thinking back, I would say it was god's will and strength that we never looked back and thought twice about what would happen to us.

The Gills were indoors. The hundred-plus mob had shattered the windowpanes and were on the verge of barging in when in true cinematic style, the lady of the house had rushed out screaming with a sword in hand. Sunil's father first asked Mrs Gill to return indoors and then turned around and let loose a stream of expletives at the mob which had retreated instantly. The following year, Jaineet Kaur Gill tied a rakhi on Sunil!

The carnage of 1984 was the end of innocence for most school-going children like Jasbinder and Priti who were students of St Xavier's. Their school was used as a relief camp and once it reopened, specific instructions were given to non-Sikh children from questioning their Sikh friends. Chandrima Ray teaches in the same school she went to as a child and has memories of those days. There was an overall sense of overcoming an unprecedented tragedy but a complete embargo on talking about it, she said.

❖ ❖ ❖ ❖

'Why burden them (the kids) with my memories?' asked Surinder Pal Singh who works in the administrative department of the Bokaro General Hospital. Yet, he smiled sardonically when asked if there had been a new dawn in the lives of those who had lived through hellish times? 'There's nothing called a new day,' he said. 'Each day is a continuation of the previous one!'

On that day in November 1984, Surinder Pal Singh's sister, Gurmeet Kaur was shot by a mob which had raided their house. Gurmeet survived but the incident had driven such a fear into the hearts of her family members that once the girl began recuperating, they relocated to Punjab. While Surinder's parents and Gurmeet stayed with relatives, his two brothers failed to find jobs in Punjab and returned to Bokaro. Surinder also witnessed his elder brother's mental anguish, who was constantly harangued by his colleagues for having survived the ordeal and had literally fled to Bhilai Steel Plant.

Meanwhile Surinder Pal Singh found a way to reconstruct his life and as general secretary of the local Riots Victims' Association, he began assisting the Misra Commission and pressed upon riot-affected families to depose for a fair rehabilitation package. During the process, Surinder Pal was shocked to discover that the identification of rioters was nearly impossible in Bokaro because none of them had a past criminal record nor where they led by local political leaders, as was the case in Delhi. Some of the observations by the Misra Commission further delineated the violence in Bokaro and most significantly that, 'while in Kanpur and Delhi, ladies were ordinarily exempted from attack,' there were 'incidents at Bokaro of the female folk being also the target of killing.'

Post the Misra Commission's recommendations, the rehabilitation measures in Bokaro enabled those who had stayed back to rebuild their lives—dependents were given jobs in the Steel Plant while widows were absorbed into the state police force. In a few years, Surinder Pal Singh also got a job, married and raised a family.

Surinder's cynicism bothered me for many days after the interview. Why had he denied the possibility of a new dawn in the lives of Sikhs in Bokaro? The answer to this was best articulated in the Misra Commission report:

> The police at Bokaro were not as ineffective as at Kanpur or Delhi. Many of the affidavits indicate that the police came and helped. The Administration actually sought the help of Central Industrial Security Force which was put into use and the situation in Bokaro was contained within 7-8 hours. The Commission takes notice of the fact that most of the incidents are subject-matter of FIRs which more or less have complete particulars. In almost every case an investigation has followed and a large number of cases have ended up in charge-sheets. As noted in another part of the Report, some of these cases are already under trial.

Although the Misra Commission report was submitted in August 1986, the police had failed to secure a single conviction in Bokaro. It was worse in Dhanbad because unlike Bokaro, the violence in the city had largely gone unnoticed from public attention. But similar to Bokaro, a number of Sikh families in Dhanbad also shifted from their homes to makeshift shelters, and later either migrated to Punjab in search of employment or moved in with relatives in other cities. Eventually when they returned to the city, disillusioned and tired of finding jobs, they found their homes and business establishments looted. The Sikhs of Dhanbad had nowhere to hide.

Thirty-two year old Sewa Singh worked as an assistant Public Relations Officer in the Sindri plant of Fertiliser Corporation of India, a short distance away from Dhanbad. On 31 October, a colleague had forewarned him about the riots and Sewa wisely returned home before dusk. But unfortunately, his mother who was visiting relatives in Chas village, was caught in the riots and was severely beaten up while her brother was killed. Despite a great personal tragedy, Sewa established the Jharkhand Sikh Welfare Society and devoted himself to the cause after the Sindri plant was closed down.

During the process of reopening criminal cases, Sewa Singh learnt that a majority of FIRs in Dhanbad had been erroneously recorded as collective complaints. Further, a large number of cases were bundled out of courts since most of the complainants were untraceable, and had migrated to Punjab. A similar complication arose while filing for compensations. The government had agreed to pay those who had registered their complaints immediately after the loss of property, which was impossible in the case of absentees.

Meanwhile in Bokaro, a reverse and shameful phenomenon was witnessed when a few Sikh families filed false or exaggerated compensation claims. A report in the *Tehelka* magazine in December 2007 stated that of the amount disbursed between April and August 2007, several families had received huge sums of money by presenting forged documents.

Strangely, Joginder Singh Johal of Dhanbad never bothered about his losses. After all he was from a privileged background—his father was none other than Sardar Darbara Singh, who was chief minister of Punjab between 1980 and 1983, and one of the main dramatis personae in the state's turbulent history.

Joginder Singh had arrived in Dhanbad in his early Twenties in 1957 and established a successful empire which included liquor retail units in Jharkhand and a three star hotel called Skylark. After a few years, the next generation stepped in and by 1984, the family controlled the entire liquor trade in south Bihar besides owning several showrooms of two-wheelers. Gradually, the Johals also built lucrative enterprises in West Bengal. But all that changed in a fraction of a second in 1984. One of Joginder's younger brothers decided to leave Dhandbad permanently and moved to faraway Tamil Nadu; and Joginder scaled down his operations in Dhanbad and Bokaro. But neither did he ever file a complaint nor seek any compensation and perhaps paid a price for his father's stature. At seventy-five, he often has a drink with his friends in the evenings but is unable to conceal the pain of a terrible loss.

Far removed from the bustle of Dhanbad, the one-time legendary and firebrand labour leader of the Marxist Coordination Committee, A K Roy lay paralysed in a tiny hut in Nuridih village. In 1984, he was the elected representative from Dhanbad and played a significant role in protecting the Sikh community during the carnage. Comrade Roy was dependant on the party cadre for his upkeep as he had donated his entire pension to the national relief fund.

Despite his inability to speak, A K Roy was extremely alert and exuded a rare innocence which is often the privilege of those who renounce the world. I was told that in January 2014, thieves had barged into his hut and decamped with the only gift he had ever accepted in his life, a marker of time—an HMT watch! I was hoping he would add to my Jharkhand chapter and asked him about the atrocities on Sikhs in Dhanbad. 'The circumstances were such,' said Roy brusquely and ended the topic. Roy's hut was the last halt in my attempt to unravel the jigsaw.

From Dhandbad, I boarded the night train to home in Delhi. As the coach hurtled through the night, the fog became a metaphor for the shroud on the carnage in Bokaro, Dhanbad and several other cities of Jharkhand...

They were terrified the moment some strangers sought directions to a toilet. When they realised that I had noticed their apprehension, the four appeared nonchalant and continued the conversation. It was after we got out of the rickety auto rickshaw which brought us back from their house that I realised—it wasn't fear but the shame of being discovered that had made them diffident.

The house which looked pretty from the outside and had a large living room, was a pretence. Once I passed through the space,  commonly known in India as the drawing room, the rest of the house was a clutter. One had to manoeuvre through dirty heaps of clothes and household goods, past a small niche which functioned as a kitchen before the toilet stuck out from the rear wall. This was the home of forty-two-year-old Mandeep Singh who lives in Kanpur with his wife, Satpal Kaur and parents, Harjit Singh and Tejinder Kaur.

We had just begun our conversation when Mandeep suddenly scampered out of the room. A few moments later, he returned holding a bawling child in his arms. The little boy's mother muttered softly, 'What can the poor boy do, after all he didn't witness the *dehshat* (horror) and does not understand why we are scared for him.' The fear was of the darkness outside; of leaving a child alone in the narrow streets; most importantly, of being attacked by murderous mobs. She continued, 'At times, it feels very claustrophobic.'

As her words died down, those written in September 1986 in the *India Today* magazine came to life as a cruel reminder of the tragedy. In the introductory blurb, Raminder Singh wrote:

> Among the most tragic—and pathetic—victims of Sikh terrorism are the Sikhs themselves—millions of Sikhs who have made their homes and livelihoods outside Punjab and have prospered because of their skills and initiative. Many of them have never even stepped inside Punjab.

The magazine further reported that the Tata Express, which linked Kanpur with Amritsar, operated four times a week carrying, 'at least two Sikh families who are moving back to Punjab with bag and baggage. Sometimes more, but almost never less.'

The visit to Kanpur brought back memories of 1984 when I was part of a three-member team assisting relief workers in the city. The rehabilitation work included collecting cash donations from citizens and representatives of donor agencies which would be deposited with the elected office bearers of the largest gurudwara in the city.

Hours before I had visited Mandeep Singh and his family in the Labour Colony tenement, I met Mokham Singh, who sat in a small office of a medium-sized, yet historically significant gurudwara in Kanpur. We began talking and he gradually took over the conversation. After a while, he was openly boastful of securing relief for several riot-affected Sikh families in Kanpur. I paused for a bit and wondered where I had seen this prosperous-looking Sikh? And it struck me a moment later. It was Mokham Singh who had taken us around Kanpur three decades ago on that unfortunate winter morning. But on that day, he presented himself as an important member of a lobby which demanded higher compensation and better rehabilitation packages for the victims of Sikh riots.

In the late 1980s, after the twin disasters of Operation Blue Star and Indira Gandhi's assassination, it had become imperative for Sikh leaders in Kanpur to enlist members from the community for leveraging with political parties. As a result, a new patron-client chain developed in the city with ordinary Sikhs at the lowest rung and political parties or their leaders at the top.

Curiously even in the pre-1984 period, Sikhs in Kanpur were not a cohesive group and consequently not a monolithic vote bank that could be delivered to a single party. For instance, during the elections held between 1957 to 1977, Kanpur was like a trade union bastion and voted for a unionist, S M Banerjee; caste and religion-based identities played a secondary role and a majority of Sikhs in Kanpur voted primarily on the basis of socio-economic affiliations.

In 1980, the Congress party emerged as a  strong political force in the city but lost its clout after several Sikh groups began veering  towards the anti-Congress front that had begun coalescing from 1987. However, in November 1990 after the fall of the Janata Dal government, Sikh groups in Kanpur  attached themselves to assorted political patrons and in large numbers to Mulayam Singh Yadav and Kanshi Ram of the Samajwadi Party (SP) and Bahujan Samaj Party (BSP), respectively.

The two lakh Sikhs were a readymade vote bank and their leaders most influential in turning the tide for any political party in UP. For instance, Mokham Singh had a support base among a small section and he influenced them to vote for the BSP, a party he joined in the early 1990s.

However, despite associating with divergent political parties, Sikh leaders in Kanpur remained united in devising a common strategy to seek higher compensation and political concessions for the riot-affected from the Centre. In 1995, the then Chief Minister of Uttar Pradesh, Mulayam Singh Yadav attempted to appease the Sikhs by altering the course of jurisprudence in a case which had its origins dating back to 1988.

❦ ❦ ❦ ❦

In 1977, Kanpur the largest city in the state of Uttar Pradesh, was hived off for administrative convenience into urban and rural districts—Kanpur Shahar and Dehat. As part of the Awadh or Oudh kingdom, the city was administered by the Raj in early nineteenth century and became the largest industrial centre in north India, earning the sobriquet of Manchester of the East. After Partition, many Sikh entrepreneurs settled in Kanpur and by the mid-Eighties, the city had an estimated Sikh population of 1.5 lakhs.

In 1984, within a span of twenty-four hours, 127 Sikhs engaged in medium to large enterprises were killed in Kanpur. As mentioned earlier, despite a number of Sikh casualties, the state government provided the Misra Commission with different terms of reference to investigate the violence in the city. As was the case in Bokaro, an inquiry into the violence in Kanpur was initiated only after Prime Minister Rajiv Gandhi signed a peace accord with Sant Harchand Singh Longowal. When the probe finally got underway, it was not to investigate "organised violence" but to probe "disturbances". Curiously, the Misra Commission in one of its earlier reports had noted that there had been allegations of "organised" violence in Kanpur but was "bound by the terms of reference" and committed to the "spontaneous outbreak of violence" theory. Later, the Nanavati Commission appointed in 2000 by the Atal Bihari Vajpayee-led NDA government was also focussed excessively on Delhi and barring occasional observations, did not probe the violence in Kanpur. Therefore, till date, the Misra Commission remains the only official reference point for understanding the violence in Kanpur.

According to the Commission, all the deaths in Kanpur had occurred between the afternoon of 31 October and the night of 1 November 1984. A large number of deaths were also reported in trains running through Kanpur but the city police had excluded these from the final tally as railway stations were not under its jurisdiction. Of the 127 deaths, post-mortems were conducted on fifty-seven bodies and the remaining seventy were termed "untraceable"—burnt, swept away or perhaps abandoned. Between 31 October and 2 November, the Kanpur police had arrested 2,316 rioters, but they were all released on bail. Therefore, by the time the Misra Commission had arrived in Kanpur to initiate a probe, most of the accused had escaped. There were no cases to register, and zero convictions for murder, arson or looting in the city. It was as if Kanpur had been wiped clean from the pool of blood in 1984....

❀ ❀ ❀ ❀

Eleven year old Mandeep Singh was a student of a reputed missionary school during the riots in Kanpur. He had witnessed his father's cycle repair shop being vandalised and his home being razed to the ground.

Mandeep's father, Harjit Singh sold his half-burnt house at a throwaway price, locked up his shop and moved to Amritsar. Recounting a similar story for the *India Today* magazine, Raminder Singh wrote, 'Half the property owned by Kanpur Sikhs has already been sold, sometimes at half the market price. No Sikh has bought land here after 1984. Not a brick has been added to houses that were being built.'

The move to Amristar proved futile for Harjit as he struggled each day to establish himself in an alien business culture. Despite the money from the sale of the house and the paltry fifty thousand rupees as compensation, he could never accumulate the working capital to stock up his fledgling shop.

One day he returned home and to his old cycle shop. But everything had changed. His two businesses had suffered huge losses and Mandeep who was now admitted to a Hindi-medium school had lost interest in academics. The years rolled by and finally, Mandeep dropped out of college and joined his father's floundering venture. The family moved frequently—from one rented house to another as house owners in Kanpur were nervous of Sikh tenants.

After the passing of a few years, around the mid-1990s, the father-son duo decided to recast the business and became cycle spare part suppliers. After several years, there was peace at home and soon Mandeep's marriage was fixed with Satpal Kaur who taught in a college.

But there was no respite for Harjit. The local police continued to treat him like a suspect and he would often be subjected to intense scrutiny in public places. Gradually, the old man became reclusive and left the family business to his son.

Mandeep told me how in the late 1980s, his father would often sit alone watching television till late at night. His eyes would mist over each time the Bajaj scooter commercial played on the screen. The rioters had torched his Bajaj scooter that day in 1984….Harjit would wait till the last lines of the jingle wafted into the empty room—*Buland Bharat ki buland tasveer* (Vibrant India's Vibrant Picture). He would then get up, switch off the television and go to bed.

---

* The setting up of the Misra Commission was a belated attempt by the Rajiv Gandhi government—the probe in Delhi and several other cities was initiated almost five months after the violence. It took another six months before the Commission's sphere of inquiry was extended to Kanpur and Bokaro. In years since, not a single government probed the anti-Sikh violence in other parts of India despite widespread attacks on trains carrying Sikh passengers and assaults in places like Coimbatore (Tamil Nadu), remote from the disturbances in Punjab. The Misra Commission conducted its proceedings behind a veil of secrecy leading to several civil rights groups' withdrawal from the inquiry. The panel resorted to semantics in its drafted brief—

probed "allegations in regard to the incidents of organised violence", to justify the investigations. The Misra Commission did not collaborate with survivors to get to the truth but remained  sceptic of their testimonies. Several writers have previously written searing indictments of the Misra Commission and argued that it was a whitewash. Manoj Mitta and H S Phoolka's *When a Tree Shook Delhi*; Jaskaran Kaur's *Twenty Years of Impunity*; Jyoti Grewal in *Betrayed by the State: The Anti-Sikh Pogrom of 1984* and Parvinder Singh's *1984: Sikhs' Kristallnacht* are a few books that examine the conduct of Misra Commission. Yet, despite its limited purview,  the  recorded testimonies of survivors before the Commission conveyed a lot more than what was unstated. This book does not claim to critically examine the Misra Commission but uses its report for the benefit of its readers.

# Eight

# The Citizens Collective

A big tree had indeed fallen, as proclaimed by the political leadership in Delhi. But it was also ensured that the ground beneath the feet of hapless Sikhs in the capital and elsewhere shuddered with the same intensity because they had to be "taught a lesson".

Dinesh Mohan, the former IIT don recalled a peculiar situation in Trilokpuri on the evening of 3 November after news that the resettlement colony had been one of the most horrific theatres of human slaughter. Pappu, the local history-sheeter had sidled up to Dinesh Mohan with information that almost fifty Sikhs were trapped in the basement of a godown in his locality. The curfew curtailed him from launching a rescue operation or else he would have secured their lives, said he to Prof Mohan.

On that evening, ascertaining the veracity of a petty criminal's claim would have invited opprobrium for the Professor. Yet, the head of the Army unit was duly approached, and after a few minutes, a truck carrying Sikhs had melted into the enveloping darkness. Once the mission was accomplished, Pappu invited

Dinesh Mohan and others for a round of drinks to celebrate a "good deed".

It wasn't as if the IIT professor had strayed into Trilokpuri as he had done two days ago with his camera in and around AIIMS to record what appeared like a mini Partition-like situation. However incredulous this may have seemed at the time, he was now part of a ginger group that had resolved to rescue Delhi from the clutches of communal thugs and had gathered in Trilokpuri.

In the aftermath of the most brutal massacre in post-independent India, it is of little consequence when and how a citizen's initiative was begun. Although largely forgotten on account of its spontaneous nature, civil society's involvement in November 1984 was extraordinary, particularly in the absence of the State. It started simply: a handful of people shocked at the enormity of a tragedy, set in motion India's biggest middle class-led relief and rehabilitation operation since Partition.

H S Phoolka was a young lawyer in his late Twenties and had escaped to Punjab with his family, vowing never to return to Delhi. Then one day, he did. 'I came back because I realised that in Delhi, there were people who were still willing to risk their existence to fight this mythic monster. We returned because in them I saw great power,' said he, one quiet Saturday afternoon in his office at the Delhi High Court.

The group assembled on the morning of 1 November by which time the city's skyline had turned grey with drifting smoke and its streets were openly managed by lumpens. Poonam Muttreja (now Executive Director of Population Fund of India) in her affidavit to Misra Commission mentioned that on that day, forty non-Sikhs had walked in a procession through some sections of Lajpat Nagar in south Delhi. What they did during the course of the march is largely forgotten except that they were faced with mobs brandishing iron rods and *trishuls* or tridents.

At some point, the group was joined by a saffron-clad duo, Swami Agnivesh (born Shyam Vepa Rao and well-known for his campaign against bonded labour) and his Arya Samaji associate, Swami Indravesh. Agnivesh's presence not only added credibility to the group, there was also the added advantage of being in the company of men in saffron clothes, which in 1984 was still associated with moral rectitude. At one place, Agnivesh even jumped onto a makeshift platform and beseeched the attackers to eschew violence and return home, but to little avail.

One year later, Ravi Chopra (who was then a key member of the Centre for Science and Environment and now the spearhead of Peoples' Science Institute, Dehradun) mentioned the involvement of two renunciates in a citizen's initiative. In an interview to the lawyer-turned-activist, Nandita Haksar and this author in May 1985 for the book, *Delhi Riots: Three Days in the Life of a Nation*, he spoke of Swami Indravesh's duplicity and highlighted how he had initially baulked at the idea of a peace march but was later coerced into joining it. In retrospect, Ravi was merely echoing what was then evident across the political spectrum—the Congress was driven by vendetta, while leaders of opposition parties had chosen silence in the face of an emerging Hindu vote bank.

On 2 November, the processionists met again and discovered that their numbers had swelled. As the group had no formal agenda on hand, they began instinctively with what seemed most imperative at the time and decided to "shake up" the State; some tried meeting leaders from political parties; a few even attempted to enter Teen Murti House forcibly where Indira's Gandhi's body lay in-state. The first so-called breakthrough came when they met Arun Nehru, then the principal aide to Rajiv Gandhi, who promised prompt action but did nothing. As events turned out later and even more recently according to fresh evidence pieced together by senior journalist, Hartosh Bal for the *Caravan* magazine in October 2014, "orders for the violence" had come from Nehru who had allegedly made the electoral rolls of Delhi's gurudwaras available to rioters.

Later that day, the citizen's group organised yet another peace march which was joined by the Janata Party president, Chandra Shekhar and several members of the party's executive committee including George Fernandes. The presence of well-known politicians lent considerable weight to the peace initiative and not only did the looting and arson abate for a short while, Chandra Shekhar and his partymen had firsthand accounts of the terrible violence. A few rioters on their way back from the railway yard outside Hazrat Nizamuddin Station accepted that they had pulled out Sikhs from express trains to kill.

In his interview, Ravi Chopra estimated that on 2 November, the group 'covered something like eight and a half kilometres in about two and a half hours,' which was a remarkable achievement in a city ravaged by hatred. That evening as dusk enveloped the capital, the group decided to strengthen their resolve and formalised the collective by naming it the Nagrik Ekta Manch (NEM). Officials of the Servants of the People Society, the organisation formed by Lala Lajpat Rai in Lahore in 1921, offered space in Lajpat Bhawan and for several weeks thereafter, the entire complex became the epicentre of relief operations. 'The bulk of the response to the formation of NEM was from largely apolitical, middle-class citizens—housewives, students, professionals—who came forward to contribute their might in restoring sanity to the scarred city. Obviously, the appeal by the initiators struck a responsive chord,' wrote Harsh Sethi (now senior consulting editor of the *Seminar* magazine), in a special issue of the *Lokayan* Bulletin, titled "Voices from a Scarred City: The Delhi Carnage in Perspective".

As the sun rose over a wintery Delhi morning on 3 November, the horror of mass murders became public for the first time—there were detailed reports in the *Indian Express* and *Jansatta* about the massacres in Trilokpuri. The volunteers of NEM, sensing an opportunity for their first official intervention, immediately headed towards Block 32 in the area.

Ravi Chopra recounted that when he went back to join the group that morning in Lajpat Bhawan, the situation had worsened in Delhi. Sikhs were huddled inside schools, colleges, police stations, on rooftops, in  basements and gurudwaras. Make-shift camps had sprung up at several places and groups of mourners were seen lamenting for their missing relatives after giving up hope for basics like food, medicines, clothes or blankets to face the chill at night. On 3 November, the NEM collected 20,000 rupees as donation and by 5 November, almost 600 volunteers had joined the outfit. Lajpat Bhawan became the site of a full-fledged rehabilitation operation.

As a key member of the Manch, Ravi Chopra began by managing the telephone which rang constantly—frantic conversations seeking details about relief operations and some enquiring about making contributions. The Bhawan's lawns were soon covered with blankets, sacks of cereals, edible oil, sugar, tea leaves, milk powder, baby food, and sanitary napkins which were loaded onto trucks which would curiously arrive every morning from unknown destinations and whose owners remained anonymous till the very end.

Within days, a full-fledged store was set up in the building's auditorium and teams of volunteers were entrusted with the task of maintaining a detailed inventory of relief material. By mid-November, the Nagrik Ekta Manch set up a Steering Committee which monitored five relief camps in Delhi besides extending support to Sikhs in several resettlement colonies. Even as Delhi was limping back to normalcy, the relief operations in Lajpat Bhawan continued to attract volunteers. The coordinators had strict instructions from the Steering Committee to refrain from making memberships mandatory but people nevertheless trooped in everyday.

One day Alok Mukhopadhyay, then head of OXFAM and one of the founding members of NEM, noticed a Sikh gentleman who arrived every morning with his wife to hand over relief material. The two struck up a conversation and as the Sikh couple readied to take leave, Alok asked the man his name. 'My name is Manmohan Singh. I work as the Governor of Reserve Bank of India,' said he and walked away. And then there were others—well known writer, Amitav Ghosh who sourced material to build temporary homes for people living in open camps; actor M K Raina who managed the transport of materials and volunteers; the now deceased publisher and newscaster, Tejeshwar Singh who took charge of logistics while veteran journalist, the late Chanchal Sarkar, coordinated with families reporting missing members.

Gradually, the Nagrik Ekta Manch also doubled up as an informal post-traumatic facility as some of its volunteers were trained professionals with past experiences in dealing with human disasters across the world. For example, in camp after camp, Sikh widows would narrate the macabre killings of their menfolk ad nauseam and I would be astounded by young volunteers who would convince them of a future beyond their immediate tragedies. Although there were no formal training modules at the collective, young women, mostly college-going students apprenticed under older volunteers while young men were expected to watch over children of widows. The concept of relief and rehabilitation extended beyond distributing baby food, clothing, medicines and shelter; Delhi needed to awaken its conscience and the Nagrik Ekta Manch, by sheer accident became its keeper. This realisation came to me late one evening when I had dropped in at a Sikh friend's house for a meal. The conversation on the table was focussed on my daily routine as a NEM volunteer. Even as I was nearing the end of my narration and paused for a breath, my friend's mother commented: 'Thank God, there is still some *insaniyat* (humanity) left in this city!'

As mentioned above, the Nagrik Ekta Manch was formed in response to State apathy and strictly functioned as a non-political, not for profit citizen's initiative. Once the relief and rehabilitation process got underway, a few NEM members suggested expanding its role to investigate the cause and nature of violence which had led to the death of 2,733 Sikhs in the Indian capital. As a result, a senior journalist called Sumanta Banerjee, the deceased civil rights activist, Smitu Kothari and Dinesh Mohan were quietly pulled out of relief operations and given charge of the assignment. Young volunteers were pressed into interviewing survivors but with a questionnaire that left little room for extrapolations.

The initial findings of the field investigations were extremely disturbing and indicated a strange pattern of uniformity. After an in-depth investigation of the matter, the core team comprising Sumanta, Dinesh Mohan and Smitu Kothari arrived at three major conclusions—first, a majority of local area leaders owing allegiance to the Congress party had led the mobs; second, the killings were carried out using three main substances namely, an inflammable white powder of undeterminable composition, kerosene or petrol and old car tyres and thirdly and most importantly, a few Congress MPs found recurring mentions— H K L Bhagat, Sajjan Kumar, Dharam Das Shastri, Jagdish Tytler, along with two metropolitan councillors, Lalit Maken and Arjun Dass. There was yet another similarity. All of them had been initiated into the Congress party by Sanjay Gandhi during the Emergency.

Chronicling every detail of the anti-Sikh riots, the findings later formed part of a  booklet titled, "Who Are The Guilty?" In relief camps and amongst riot survivors, it was popularly known as the *kali kitaab* or "black book" not only because it had a black front cover but it listed the names of politicians who had allegedly led the rioters in the aftermath of Indira Gandhi's assassination. The findings were later published and formally released as a report by two of India's largest civil liberty groups, the PUCL and PUDR. This intervention, albeit correctly as the report required formal ratification, led to a minor controversy amongst some members of the Nagrik Ekta Manch who were loathe to political association especially if there was a risk of being labelled "anti-establishment".

The other contentious issue was about listing the names of rioters in the booklet, which some NEM members felt amounted to conjecture, while others argued that it shifted the onus of a final ratification on the government. This opinion was further buttressed by the fact that several names in the report were identifiable only by their aliases—for instance, Papita, Bihari

Dhobi, Massa (opium dealer), Mukri Master (tailor), Punju, Abbas ka Damaad (meaning son-in-law of Abbas) and so on.

Although "Who Are The Guilty?" acknowledged 'the volunteers of the Nagrik Ekta Manch and many others who by their dedicated work made possible the investigation and publication of this report,' it made many within NEM's ranks question the association with PUCL-PUDR. As long as the Manch was focussed on relief measures, it was perceived to be a spontaneous citizen's initiative in support of a humanitarian cause. But once the report was made public, it acquired an anti-Congress image, which challenged the basic premise of the movement.

However there were also others who felt that NEM would lose its relevance unless it had a strong political backing and after several deliberations, Jaya Jaitley, one of its key members, took the lead and formed the Peoples' Relief Committee as an initiative of the Janata Party with former Vice President and one-time Chief Justice of India, M Hidayatullah, as its chairperson. But it was a non-starter and failed to draw the requisite number of volunteers. Over time, other groups were formed as well— for instance, the Indian Express group of newspapers which raised donations and also set up a Relief Fund for the widows of 1984 but it strictly operated as a funding group and sought out initiatives that were apolitical.

By December 1984, most NEM volunteers returned to their routines; relief camps were vacated and the survivors had begun on their long road to recovery. It was first suggested that NEM should be made a permanent body, but there were few takers for it; there was also  talk about NEM transforming into a funding agency like OXFAM, but finally, nothing came to fruition. However, the Manch did not have the option of closing down operations as large number of victims were still dependent on its volunteers for relief measures, of which the most important was the rehabilitation of widows. Eventually, it outsourced  its relief operations to reputed NGOs like Saheli and

Ankur by delegating them  to set up facilities for the women and children of 1984.

But in one of its last-ditch efforts at rehabilitation  work, the Manch took up the  rebuilding of poor Sikhs' homes  in areas such as  Trilokpuri, Sultanpuri, Mongolpuri, and Kalyanpuri and assisted them in the resumption of their professional work. But the end was nigh and in the  next couple of months, the Manch scaled down operations and shifted out of its office from Lajpat Nagar in south Delhi. Eventually what survived was a bank account with a few thousand rupees but more importantly, memories that lasted a lifetime.

And then in late 2014, a new generation of volunteers took the lead (with support from Aman Biradari, founded by Harsh Mander in collaboration with Tejeshwar Singh Memorial Trust) to work amongst the survivors of the 1984 carnage in  Tilak Vihar. A couple of months later in March 2015, this group formally revived the Nagrik Ekta Manch  which despite its association with a few old-timers, is a new beginning.

For many like this author, the experience with the Nagrik Ekta Manch was a rite of passage and virtually decided the future course of one's life. For instance, writer and artist Shuddhabrata Sengupta who was a student of class eleven in Springdales School in 1984 and spent several days volunteering with relief groups. The following year, this sixteen-year-old boy was part of another group which conducted a summer camp at IP College for the children of Tilak Vihar. But after teaching, playing, singing and dancing with the children of the riots, Sengupta may have lost faith in the idea of an idyllic childhood and a Republic called India but he forged a new form of kinship. Along with Safina Uberoi, Shuddhabrata became part of a circle of five friends who named their group, *Panj Pyare*, or the beloved five!

Meanwhile NEM provided Jaya Srivastava an identity that she had denied herself as the wife of a corporate executive. 'I became politically conscious because of my involvement with NEM,' said Jaya, who had worked with the women and children in the slums of Delhi. After a long pause, she added, 'I owe my understanding of life to those women who allowed me to interact with them.'

Unlike several others who had walked into Lajpat Bhawan of their own volition to participate in the collective, Jaya Srivastava was introduced to the Manch by her son. Her initial response was one of shock and bewilderment which persisted even after she was sent off to Nanaksar Ashram in east Delhi to manage the relief camp. As she described to me later, 'These were evolutionary phases in my socio-political awareness.' For example, the realisation of what dignity meant for the young and economically-backward widows with children when they turned down offers of adoption from the rich. For several nights thereafter, Jaya would lie awake in bed. Her husband of more than two decades would also keep awake, troubled about the sudden change in his wife.

Jaya Srivastava's son, Aseem (see chapter One, Doomsday Delhi) remembers how his father had reacted. 'Initially there was an undercurrent of tension,' he said. 'We were essentially four strong individuals but over time we overcame the crisis. I always think of my family as three rocks and an ocean swirling in between—that's my mother... they clashed but I think my parents resolved it as amicably and maturely as two people can. My father changed—he just became a lot more understanding and tolerant than we knew him to be...'

However, Jaya Srivastava was not the only one. Lalita Ramdas, wife of the former Indian Naval Chief, Admiral (Retd) Laxminarayan Ramdas, underwent a similar experience when her husband walked into their home one evening and found it taken over by NEM volunteers! Lalita had previously been involved with various social movements on issues of gender, environment and education and was also instrumental in setting up Ankur, a society for alternatives in education. Therefore it wasn't as if her husband was unused to her professional life but what he experienced that evening was palpably different! The Admiral was reminded of his father who had sheltered a Muslim colleague and his four children for almost two months during the Partition in 1947.

After spending decades planning and executing war games in the seas, the Admiral joined the Pakistan-India People's Forum for Peace and Democracy in 1998 and participated in a march to protest against India's nuclear test in Pokhran. A decade and a half later in 2013, Admiral Ramdas became the Lokpal of the Aam Aadmi Party (AAP) at a time when other retired service chiefs and officers were jostling to join the Bharatiya Janata Party or BJP. According to Lalita, 'The involvement with relief and rehabilitation of survivors was a defining moment for a large number of people in a fundamental way.'

It's been more than thirty years after the virtual "death" of the Nagrik Ekta Manch, but some of its members still lament its passing with a great sense of remorse. While recalling those times, Alok Mukhopadhyay said to me, 'Firstly, despite the pogrom, the system was still not so rotten and moreover, it was easier to forge bonds even amongst people from diverse backgrounds…'

Without resorting to the romance of nostalgia which is often the prerogative of old revoltionaries, Nagrik Ekta Manch was a vehicle of self discovery for many and shall remain a significant catalyst in the process of change in post-independent India.

# Nine

# The Art of 1984

The world over, socio-political change compels creativity. At times as part of a homogenous cultural movement, or at other times, sporadically, as individual efforts. For instance, the cultural upsurge witnessed in the aftermath of Partition is widely acknowledged as the most remarkable example of artistic flourish in the sub-continent. Saadat Hasan Manto, the most stellar example of the period, migrated and eventually died in Pakistan, but continues to stir tragic memories on either side of the border. And then there were others—Khushwant Singh, Rajinder Singh Bedi, Amrita Pritam, Bhisham Sahni, Intizar Hussain, Kartar Singh Duggal, and K A Abbas who contributed brilliantly to the genre of "partition literature" spanning various languages like, Hindi, Urdu, Punjabi and English.

Curiously, when viewed from the prism of a complete obliteration of land, identity and dignity, the Punjab imbroglio and the riots of 1984 somehow failed in stimulating a body of outstanding work either in literature or the arts. This is not to deny the artists their contribution—but it happened in spurts and therefore failed to be a robust part of contemporary literary history.

I discovered how this phenomenon had striking similarities with the two partitions on the eastern side of the sub-continent in 1947 and 1971—Bengali literature, like its cinema, not only treated the plight of refugees as a mere backdrop, it made no attempts to chronicle the dispossession of Muslims from West to East Bengal.

Amandeep Sandhu, the noted writer, journalist and critic, wrote about the collective failure of the period in an article for *The Hindu* on 1 February 2014, as follows:

> …stalwarts like Amrita Pritam and Kartar Singh Duggal were too close to the violence to write about it and Punjab-based writers Gurdial Singh, Jaswant Singh Kanwal and Dileep Kaur Tiwana were too far removed from the violence to write from experiential knowledge. In any case the gap remained; their silence a black hole in the living room of Punjabi language and literature.

However, a significant reason for artists to have fallen into the allegorical black hole is while there was a semblance of an "intellectual closure" during Partition, the anti-Sikh episode remained unresolved and therefore failed to coalesce as a cultural movement. Moreover the unrest in Punjab lacked empathy even amongst victims who were separated both geographically and culturally across different parts of the country.

With the only established truth of State's complicity in the 1984 riots, the focus during the period was primarily on non-fiction writing involving investigation and analysis (there were a few instances of fiction writing in Punjabi, of which later). For instance, Uma Chakravarti and Nandita Haksar's *Delhi Riots: Three Days in the Life of a Nation* (for which this author conducted several interviews), was remarkable in that it documented the testimonies of not only the survivors of the anti-Sikh pogrom but also volunteers who assisted them in various relief camps. Interestingly, in the case of a few non-fiction writers, the lines between activism and ethnographic surveys were often blurred, as was with Dr Veena Das, whose exemplary writing on the women and children of 1984 was alongside her rehabilitation work in relief camps. She later wrote a brilliant essay titled, "Our Work to Cry; Your Work to Listen", highlighting the agony of Shanti (see chapter Three, The Horror!The Horror!) and her two pre-pubescent daughters.

❀ ❀ ❀ ❀

It is well known that mainstream Hindi cinema is largely viewed as escapist and this despite the fact that even as early as post-Independence, "Nehruvian" ideas had impacted several filmmakers who had lived through the agony of Partition. The most obvious example was B R Chopra's *Naya Daur* (1957) and yet another from the same stable four years later in 1961, directed by his younger sibling, Yash Chopra. *Dharmputra* is often classified as the first film on the theme of Partition (albeit much delayed), but it was more about Nehruvian secularism than the birth of two nations. Although the film won the National Award for Best Hindi Film and the Filmfare for Best Dialogues in 1963, it was declared a commercial flop. As a result, it became a considered viewpoint that Indians were not ready to witness the gore of Partition on the big screen and perhaps deterred other filmmakers from exploring the theme. It took another decade for M S Sathyu to make the brilliantly crafted *Garam Hawa* in 1973 followed by *Pinjar,* which was directed by Chandra Prakash Dwivedi thirty years later in 2003.

In 1986 when *Buniyaad* became one of the most iconic serials on the government-run Doordarshan, it was felt that the establishment was finally ready to explore the history of Partition. It was followed a year later by another powerful telefilm called *Tamas* or Darkness, by the well-known director Govind Nihalani. Although both were widely acclaimed and stood out amidst the shoddy run-of-the-mill dramas on the state-run television channel, the timing of Partition-centric themes clearly pointed towards the government's attempts to eclipse the shame of 1984.

In many ways, the 1984 carnage also triggered a renewed interest in Partition as was evidenced in the case of Veena Das and later Urvashi Butalia, the feminist-publisher. In *The Other Side of Silence*, she acknowledged that the memories of Partition were 'rekindled by the repetition of violence against the Sikh community.' This was also true of some Punjabi fiction writers who converted their personal agonies into literary works in 1984. For instance, Gulzar Singh Sandhu who witnessed a mob chasing a hapless taxi driver near his house in south Delhi and wrote a "Mantoesque" story called *Din Divi Lut* or Daylight Dacoity about a Sikh's turban and unshorn hair, which was a recurring tragedy during the riots. (The Sahitya Akademi award-winning author was however best known for his short story titled, *Gods on Trial*, which formed part of an anthology of Partition Stories from Punjab, edited by Khushwant Singh.) In another stunning story titled, *To Be Mother, To Be Wife*, Sandhu alternated between the dilemma of two women caught in the vortex of 1984.

Yet another reason for the silence in the realm of story telling during the post-1984 period was because even well known Punjabi fiction writers like Ajeet Cour chose non-fiction as the preferred oeuvre. This form had yielded ground from the late 1970s-early 1980s in reaction to strictures imposed during the Emergency but saw a resurgence after Cour wrote "November 1984" which masqueraded as a short story but clearly belonged to the genre of faction, detailing an eye witness's account of the violence against Sikhs in 1984. Cour's sudden inability to write fiction was best explained by her daughter and celebrated painter, Arpana Caur who voiced the collective pain of artists by questioning the compulsion to paint: 'What was there to paint? Everything was so dismal. Nobody cared.' The hopelessness in Arpana was not merely that of an uninspired artist but primarily because of her deep involvement with Sikh widows in relief camps. It was only much later that Arpana resumed painting and produced a series called "The World Goes On", which was both intriguing and thematically dark, portraying water as a symbol of death. And she was not alone as two of her peers, Vivan Sundaram and Manjit Bawa also showcased riot-centric themes while working alongside the victims of 1984.

It was almost as if Amitav Ghosh, flush from the success of *The Circle of Reason,* had found a new calling in the aftermath of the Sikh riots in 1984. Like most Indians of his generation born a decade after Independence, while Ghosh had inherited the memories of Partition through his family, his exposure to the anti-Sikh pogrom while volunteering for the Nagrik Ekta Manch (NEM) was clearly manifest in *The Shadow Lines*, which he acknowledged in an interview to the *Outlook* magazine in September 2013:

> What the events of 1984 made me think of was the way in which my life has always been enmeshed in riots. A long part of this book also comes directly from my memories of a riot in Dhaka in 1964 when I was eight years old—it is one of the central scenes in the book—and of the same riot, its mirror image, happening in Calcutta.

When asked what made him travel back in time to 1964, Amitav Ghosh said that although globally, great attention is given to 'conflicts like war, for example, the Indo-Chinese war of 1962, but 1964 had completely vanished from public memory.' In a way, *The Shadow Lines* was Ghosh's attempt to keep the memories of sectarian strife alive. In an essay for the *New Yorker* in 1995, Amitav Ghosh wrote:

> Of the year's (1984) many catastrophes, the sectarian violence following Mrs Gandhi's death had the greatest effect on my life. Looking back, I see that the experiences of that period were profoundly important to my development as a writer; so much so that I have never attempted to write about them until now.

Although a couple of years younger and also grossly less accomplished as a writer in comparison to Ghosh, 1984 was a continuum of the macabre violence that I had witnessed while covering the communal riots in Meerut (Uttar Pradesh) in 1982. Almost a decade later, Ghosh articulated why the 1984 riots had had a cataclysmic impact on several minds:

> Like many other members of my generation, I grew up believing that mass slaughter of the kind that accompanied the Partition of India and Pakistan, in 1947, could never happen again. How wrong innumerable Indians had been!

A few weeks after his encounter with the survivors of 1984, Amitav Ghosh decided to write his book and said it would be,

> influenced by my experiences, but I could see no way of writing directly about those events without recreating them as a panorama of violence—"an aesthetic phenomenon" as (Bosnian writer Dzevad) Karahasan was to call it. At the time, the idea seemed obscene and futile; of much greater importance were factual reports of the testimony of the victims. But these were already being done by people who were, I knew, more competent than I could be.

Amitav Ghosh was convinced that fictionalising truth amounted to creative deception and deftly avoided the chronology of events. As a result, *The Shadow Lines* is not an "1984 book", but has a symbiotic relationship with Partition and communal violence in different parts of India and elsewhere. Ghosh had obviously made a conscious choice and noted that he was not alone as 'several others who took part in that (protest) march went on to publish books, yet nobody, so far as I know, has ever written about it except in the passing.'

Although Amitav Ghosh skipped writing a "1984 novel" but in response to Operation Blue Star and the riots post Indira Gandhi's assassination, the "Sikh novel" staged a definite comeback. A significant offshoot of popular literature in the Sikh community, the genre traces its history to Bhai Vir Singh who was a prolific writer of the late nineteenth and early twentieth century. A few decades later, Punjabi literature underwent yet another change and the focus shifted from community-centric themes to shared heritages of Hindus and Sikhs during and after the riots in 1947.

The revival of the "Sikh novel" during the Eighties was therefore quite simply a throwback to the challenges faced by the community in post-Partition India. C Christine Fair in her paper, "The Novels of Bhai Vir Singh and the Imagination of Sikh Identity, Community and Nation" attributed the resurgence to the central message in Bhai Vir Singh's "Sikh novel" as,

> martyrdom and valour would eventually come to the fruition with the establishment of Khalsa Raj under Maharaja Ranjit Singh...Faced with the Mughal intentions to annihilate the Khalsa, Vir Singh narrated how the Khalsa Singhs, by tenaciously clinging to their Khalsa identity, survive extinction.

This sentiment found ready support not only from a large section of the Sikh diaspora but also from within the country, and parallels were readily drawn between the Mughals and the ruling Congress government; while Raja Ranjit Singh became a euphemism for a future government of Khalistan. The three novels of Vir Singh that were translated and reprinted several times during the insurgency in Punjab were, *Sundri*, *Bijai Singh* and *Satwant Kaur*, with women as the main protagonists who had, as Fair elaborated,

> similar ideological agendas and historical contexts...
> all of which were coincident with Singh Sabha
> objectives, including encouraging Sikhs to embrace

their heroic and important past, expunge corruption
from their religious practice, and embrace 'orthodox'
Sikh teachings and cultivate the Punjabi language as
the sacred language of the Sikhs.

According to Christine Fair, at the height of unprecedented
international support for a separate Sikh nation, Bhai Vir
Singh's writings succeeded in 're-imagining of the transnational
diasporic Sikh world,' and 'these novels helped to redefine the
boundaries of the Sikh community at a time when boundaries
were increasingly being challenged.' This was also due to the
projection of stereotypes in his works: Muslims are rapists
and killers; Hindus are effeminate but can always partake of
the *amrit* and become a Singh; how strong female characters
behave like "Singhs" reflecting the author's viewpoint that
women must mirror their male counterparts and not just be the
carriers of a race.

Although it is difficult to establish if Bhai Vir Singh influenced
other writers to adapt the jingoistic fervour in their works, but
Ajit Rahi's *Nadar Shah Dee Vapisi* drew parallels between the
November 1984 carnage with episodes of violence against Sikhs
at different points in history. Or filmmaker and novelist Buta
Singh Shaad who linked the past to the present in his novel, *Tera
Kiya Mitha Lage*, by intertwining the tragedy faced by a family
in 1947 and later, in 1984.

While analysing the 1984-centric literature, Amandeep
Sandhu also made a special mention of *Wah Tera Chehra*, a 1990
Hindi novel by Tejinder. The book is often quoted in the context
of a deep prejudice manifested by the domiciles of the state against
those who left Punjab after migrating from Pakistan; a price
they paid for abandoning their *pind* or village which was now
home after the one they had left behind in Pakistan. Although
there were several other literary works that used the politics of
a turbulent Punjab as its backdrop, those with a direct reference
to 1984 had a far greater recall—for instance, *Jalta Hua Gulab*
published by Tarsem Gujral in 2002 about unemployed Hindu

and Sikh youth joining the extremist fringe; or the repeated editions of *Kala November*, an anthology of stories based on the theme of violence against Sikhs.

In the literary context of 1984, one of the most interesting observations was made by Prabhsahay Kaur, the human rights lawyer and daughter of H S Phoolka. According to her, the character of Dylan Singh Shekhawat in Anuja Chauhan's best-selling novel, *Those Pricey Thakur Girls* was based on Rahul Bedi, the journalist who was amongst the first to unearth the massacres in Trilokpuri and whose reports served as reference points for several legal proceedings during the period. The reason Prabhsahay found similarities was in *Those Pricey Thakur Girls,* Dylan is an idealistic journalist who works for a paper with "Truth, Balance, Courage" as its motto and Bedi, it may be recalled worked for the *Indian Express* during 1984 whose motto is "Journalism of Courage".

When I mentioned this to Rahul Bedi, he was pleasantly surprised to know that he had inspired the male protagonist in a bestseller; Anuja Chauhan however accepted that although she had researched several newspaper reports of the period, the character of Dylan was a mere coincidence. 'It was all there because you couldn't write about Delhi in the 1980s and not mention the anti-Sikh riots.' A similar sentiment was shared by yet another writer, Jaspreet Singh, in an interview with *The Times of India* in October 2013 apropos his novel titled, *Helium*. 'One does not decide to visit 1984. 1984 keeps visiting us. It is the return of repressed, re-emerging memories triggered by current events,' he said. The novel described by noted Canadian writer, Mark Antony Jarman as a "tour de force", is the poignant journey of a young man called Raj who comes to terms with his father's culpability in the violence of 1984.

❈ ❈ ❈ ❈

In the history of contemporary Punjabi cinema, the only noteworthy attempt at showcasing the state's militant phase was a film called, *Mera Punjab* (1994). However it was widely speculated that even this valiant effort at realism by Darshan Bagga was mere propaganda, supported by the then Director General of Police, K P S Gill. At the other end of the spectrum, in the realm of commercial cinema was *Maachis* (1996), which undoubtedly stood out for its thematic treatment of the period, but its director Gulzar insisted that his film was a "human love story, set in the Punjab of turmoil and militancy", and later moves to the neighbouring state of Himachal Pradesh. When seen from the prism of a romance set in Punjab of the Eighties, *Maachis* is a remarkable story of love and longing but Gulzar somehow seemed to have meandered off his chosen path as he juxtaposes the political narrative of Punjab with the pogrom in Delhi and other cities.

Similarly, if Safina Uberoi's documentary, *My Mother India* explored the question of identity, younger filmmakers like Teenaa Kaur Pasricha, focussed on how 1984 impacted ordinary individuals. While Uberoi's rediscovery of the self has been mentioned earlier in the book, Pasricha was motivated by a clutch of sad childhood stories narrated by her mother—how her uncle on board a train in October 1984 was spared after he had meekly acquiesced to have his hair cut by a bunch of hoodlums.

Shonali Bose was only nineteen in the autumn of 1984 and was working in relief camps along with friends, classmates and teachers when she met the teacher-turned-activist Mita Bose who had taken in Babli and her sister after they were hounded by relatives for the compensation money (see chapter Three, The Horror! The Horror!). The story of Babli and the futile attempts by Mita Bose in putting her up for adoption resulted in a beautiful film called *Amu* which won the National Award in 2005 for the Best Film in English and serves as an important cinematic document for its treatment of a complex web of personal relationships. Most importantly, the reason why Shonali Boses's *Amu* is a definite 1984 film is because of its backdrop which showcased the actual theatres of violence in the city.

In 2013, a young filmmaker called Shubhashish Bhutiani made an impressive debut with a twenty-minute short film titled, *Kush* and proved how 1984 continued to be relevant after twenty-nine years. The film (originally made for his diploma course at the School of Visual Arts, New York) made it to the Oscar shortlist for live action short films after bagging the Orizzonti award for Best Short Film at the prestigious Venice Film Festival. *Kush* was based on a true account of a teacher's struggle to protect a lone Sikh student in a group of ten year olds during a field trip in 1984. In one of his interviews, the debutant filmmaker made a special mention of how during the screening of his film, overseas audiences had needed no local backgrounders for understanding the violence or the grief of 1984. The triumph of *Kush* was primarily in its ability to universalise the fear associated with communal violence.

Meanwhile the 30th anniversary of the Sikh genocide coincided with the boom of multiplex theatres in India and along with the "100 crores box office phenomenon" in popular Hindi cinema, there was a huge surge of films on the subject. The first in the long list was *Dilli 1984* (2014), based on the true story of Jagdish Kaur (well known for her unrelenting pursuit against senior Congress leader, Sajjan Kumar), who had lost her husband, a son and three brothers in the mayhem and was left to fend for a six-year-old son and three daughters aged thirteen, eleven and nine. As the film raised obvious and uncomfortable questions about the ruling government's involvement in the riots, it was subsequently banned by the Central Board of Film Certification (CBFC).

A few weeks before *Dilli 1984*, yet another Punjabi film was blocked under strict instructions from the government. Titled *Kaum De Heere* or The Community's Pride (also Diamonds—or Gems—of the Community), the film glorified Indira Gandhi's assassins and was banned in India one day before its scheduled release in August 2014. Ravinder Ravi, the film's director accused the authorities of a bias because he had refused to "justify or clear the government's stand on Operation Blue Star". In another interview to the *Hindustan Times* in August 2014, Ravi claimed that the CBFC had objected to the title of the film because it referred to Indira Gandhi's assassins as *Heere* or Gems. He also contested CBFC's claim that the "government side was not shown" and retorted, 'When films or documentaries are made and funded by the government, do they show our side of the opinion?' In March 2014, the film was reviewed yet again but failed to get a clearance after the censor board's Chief Executive Officer, Rakesh Kumar was alleged to have accepted a bribe for certifying the film. Despite the controversies, the film had a fabulous run in the overseas market and was lapped up by the Sikh diaspora especially in Europe, United States, Australia and Canada.

But one of the most dramatic instances of banning involved an innocuous film called *Sadda Haq* which was a fictional account of an ace hockey player whose life transforms dramatically in the aftermath of 1984. In early 2012, the film ran into trouble with the CBFC and after several hurdles, including the script which was found to be objectionable by the authorities, the Shiromani Gurudwara Prabandhak Committee (SGPC) finally ratified the film. Meanwhile, the Akali Dal government along with its ally, the Bharatiya Janata Party or BJP, proscribed the film in Punjab in anticipation of communal tensions in the state. Curiously, the neighbouring states of Haryana and Chandigarh also followed suit despite being governed by the Congress party. In a span of a few weeks, a mediocre film had succeeded in creating a a political brouhaha—the Akalis and members of the SGPC fought openly; some of the radical groups in the state jumped into the fray and criticised the Chief Minister Prakash Singh Badal and his colleagues for belittling the SGPC and other Sikh institutions. In the following round, the SGPC not only withdrew its support to *Sadda Haq* but also objected to a song in the film by Jaswinder Singh Bains aka Jazzy B which eulogised the greatness of Guru Gobind Singh with the likes of Jarnail Singh Bhindranwale, Balwant Singh Rajoana and Jagtar Singh Hawara. Eventually after a long drawn out legal battle, the film was released with an 'A' certification.

However the eponymous, *Punjab 1984,* one of the most expensive Punjabi films made at the whopping cost of seven crores not only had a smooth sailing with the censor board but also made a killing at the box office. The film starred Diljit Dosanjh, a popular Punjabi actor, singer and television presenter as well as Kirron Kher, the well-known actress and wife of one-time CBFC Chairman, Anupam Kher, and opened with a record 1.41 crores on the first day.

After a slew of mediocre but controversial films, as the 30th anniversary of the anti-Sikh riots drew to a close, there arrived a beautifully crafted play from a long distance away in America titled, "Kultar's Mime". Based on a poem by a young Sikh poet and community activist called Sarbpreet Singh, the play incorporated several elements of Hebrew poet, Haim Nahman Bialik's *In The City Of Slaughter* about the three-day genocide of Jews in Kishinev, Russia. In a month synonymous with the killing of thousands on the streets of Delhi, when I watched the play in October 2014, it struck me how 1984 had succeeded in stimulating a man who was far removed from the tragedy but strongly exhorted the audiences to never forget the injustices of history.

Perhaps this was what had prompted the novelist, Shovon Chowdhury to start a Facebook page called, The Trilokpuri Incident, in March 2013. A typical post rambled along till one got to the end of it:

> "We never have sweets anymore," says Gurdeep. "Even if people offer, we don't take."

> She is in her thirties. She was a child at the time of the disappearances. As witnesses, children are not always reliable, but I will leave no stone unturned.

> "Are you suffering from diabetes?" I ask.

> I can understand her plight. I too am diabetic. I had too many sweets when I was young, and one day my body told me that my quota was finished.

> "I don't think so," says Gurdeep, "We can't afford it. But at that time, everyone said we were distributing sweets. That was their excuse. Since then, we never have any."

> "What happened when they thought you distributed sweets?" I ask.

> "Nothing," she says, and goes back into her shack.

# Ten

# The Circle of Politics

It is sad when a nation celebrating freedom from imperial forces, readies itself to lament with equal vigour in its immediate aftermath. By end-August 1947, Delhi had become a transit port for approximately 1,30,000 refugees—Hindus and Sikhs who had escaped from Pakistan and Muslims who were queuing up to leave India for the "Promised Land". Initially, Delhi's population of 9,50,000 had shown a considerable decrease due to the mass exodus of 3,33,000 Muslims to Jinnah's land, but it was soon evened out with the arrival of 5,00,000 non-Muslim refugees into the city.

The capital registered its highest decadal growth between 1941–51; Delhi changed, evidenced even in seemingly insignificant alterations. For instance, Qarol Bagh, a bustling commercial and residential area beyond the western fringe of the posh Connaught Place, became Karol Bagh—the change in spelling necessitated by a phonetic difference in Urdu and Hindi. This was just one of the signs of how a predominantly Indo-Islamic city was metamorphosing into a Punjabi town.

Nearly forty years later, Delhi was forced to change its character yet again after being overrun by the anti-Sikh riots, which was followed by a wave of migrants from Uttar Pradesh and Bihar.

What was once the citadel of imperial pomp was reduced to a desolate meeting ground for refugees from Pakistan and Muslims from villages, towns and cities of north India. In Delhi, large number of Muslims abandoned their homes in several localities and joined communities like the Meos, Momins and Mapillas in Purana Qila, Humayun's Tomb, Jamia Millia Islamia, sundry *qabristans* (graveyards) and even sought shelter in residences of eminent leaders of the community including, Maulana Abul Kalam Azad and Rafi Ahmed Kidwai. In an atmosphere of fear and uncertainty, individual identities became irrelevant and they huddled together as a monolithic block of Muslim refugees, hoping for  some information from the Pak Transfer Office in "L" Block, Connaught Place.

In retrospect, the situation in 1947 was a precursor to 1984 as displaced Sikhs and Hindus from across the border took refuge in swathes of wasteland, in hastily-built tenements close to the New Delhi railway station, at Kingsway (the word Camp was suffixed to the locality thereafter), the fourteenth-century fort in Tughlaqabad and the foregrounds of the Lal Qila or Red Fort etc. In a deluge myth-like situation, the resilience to cope with emotional distress was severely challenged. Well known author Krishna Sobti, herself a settler, recalled a particular gent arriving from across the border with his life's possession in a satchel and refusing to utter a word for two days. On 15 August 1947, when trays laden with sweets were passed around in Delhi, the refugees slunked away, said Krishna Sobti—they had no reasons to rejoice.

Neither did the administration of Delhi  which was faced with a catastrophe and crumbled under the weight of the additional burden. The Central Refugees Relief Committee had a mammoth task on hand but in a first instance of its kind, ordinary citizens were mobilised by three women—Sucheta Kripalani, Sushila Nayar and Subhadra Joshi who set up the first volunteer force to assist refugees and riot victims. Yet another woman who stood out for her remarkable work during the period was Begum Anees Kidwai, whose husband (the younger brother of Rafi Ahmed Kidwai) was killed in Mussoorie during the riots. At the bidding of the Mahatma, Begum Kidwai worked relentlessly in refugee camps convincing Muslims to stay back in India.

Despite a hiatus of four decades in the history of communal riots in post-Independent Delhi, the engagement of citizens groups in the aftermath of the anti-Sikh pogrom was not without a precedent. In more ways than one, the inception of the Nagrik Ekta Manch or NEM, post the 1984 riots had its genesis in 1947. Even as Sucheta Kripalani, Subhadra Joshi and Sushila Nayar went about the rehabilitation work in camps, politically motivated groups like the Hindu Sahitya Samiti, Hindu Mahasabha and Gurudwara Prabandhak Committee propped up Hindu settlers into the abandoned homes of Muslims and drove out families that had stayed back. By now Delhi was a tinderbox waiting to go up in flames.

The several uncanny and unfortunate similarities between 1947 and 1984 notwithstanding, a significant factor in a newly independent India was the presence of a man called Mahatma Gandhi. In early January 1948, he embarked on what was destined to be his last fast unto death, to awaken the "inner voice of Indians" and stop the communal mayhem in Delhi. The Mahatma was particularly distressed that Dr Zakir Hussain (who later became India's third President and was Vice Chancellor of Jamia Millia Islamia) feared for his life and felt constrained in Delhi's vicious atmosphere. In a strange coincidence, two prominent Sikhs in 1984—the Indian President, Giani Zail Singh and iconic writer, scholar and journalist, Khushwant Singh—were forced to be fugitives in Delhi, one in Rashtrapati Bhawan and the other at a diplomat's residence.

Gandhi's assassination on 30 January 1948 jolted the nation's conscience and halted the mindless violence that swept through the streets of Delhi for several months. But the city never regained its original character despite the fact that while large-scale immigration of Muslims continued, almost

1,00,000 were held back on the promise of a secular state. Yet, the change in Delhi's demographic map was soon evident: from 33.2 per cent of the city's population in 1941, Muslims in 1951 accounted for a meagre 5.7 per cent, and were mainly concentrated in the northern, central and north-eastern parts of the city. In the next decade however, the two predominant minority communities of Muslims and Sikhs accounted for 13.6 per cent of the city's population and their numbers kept rising steadily at every subsequent headcount in 1961, 1971, 1981, 1991 and 2001 (figures for 2011 were yet to be released at the time of writing this book). Yet, Gandhi's promise of a secular polity was turned into a farce because not a single political party took the onus of ensuring a parliamentary representation for Delhi's religious minorities.

By the time the first general elections were held in 1951-52, social identity, encompassing religion and caste had become imperative for the electoral strategies of every political party. Several Muslims who had stayed back in Delhi altered their physical appearance, reminiscent of Sikhs changing their identities after November 1984. Although the Congress was ostensibly opposed to the pursuance of communal politics, the party fielded Muslim candidates from constituencies that had a sizeable number from the community. For instance, the then Minister of Education and a stalwart of the freedom movement, Maulana Abul Kalam Azad was fielded from Rampur in Uttar Pradesh. In Delhi, the situation was far worse, and in what seemed like an "election-paranoia", none of the political parties fielded a single Muslim candidate from the 4 seats.

Finally after three decades, Sikandar Bakht became the first Muslim from Delhi to enter the Lok Sabha in 1977 as a Janata Party nominee. His political career was however riddled with ironies. Bhakt was initiated into politics by Subhadra Joshi during her involvement with the rehabilitation of refugees in the post-Partition period. In the late Sixties, when the Congress party split into two factions—one led by the Syndicate and the other by Indira Gandhi—Subhadra Joshi remained loyal to the latter while her protégé broke ranks and joined the rebels' Congress (O). For the one-time pupil, the injustices of Emergency in 1975, particularly Sanjay Gandhi's forced sterilisation of Muslim men, proved to be extremely potent campaign material and he vanquished Subhadra Joshi in a one-sided election in which the Muslims voted en bloc for the Janata Party.

In a complete volte face, Sikander Bakht joined the Bharatiya Janata Party or BJP in 1980 and was faced with a vicious campaign from his own party men after they raked up a curious detail about his personal life (the *Organiser* magazine, the official RSS mouthpiece had railed against him for marrying a Hindu girl in 1952). Sikandar Bakht never made it to the Lok Sabha after 1977 and by 1985 all the major political parties discontinued the occasional practise of nominating Muslim candidates in the capital.

The Sikhs were treated no differently either. Charanjit Singh (owner of Pure Drinks, a company set up by his father, Mohan Singh) was the first Sikh in Delhi to be fielded by the Congress party in 1977 but lost the elections owing to the wave of resentment against his leader and Prime Minister, Indira Gandhi for the atrocities during the Emergency in 1975–76.

Charanjit Singh was fabulously wealthy and entered politics on the strength of his financial clout as the franchise holder of Coca Cola. Khushwant Singh in *Truth, Love and a Little Malice: An Autobiography* wrote that unlike his father, Charanjit Singh harboured strong political ambitions and his largesse earned him the presidentship of the New Delhi Municipal Council (NDMC) as he had 'befriended Mrs Gandhi and her family. He provided them with cars and cash whenever and whatever purpose they needed it.' Three years later, in 1980, on the recommendation of Indira Gandhi, Charanjit Singh was once again nominated as the Congress party's candidate for the Lok Sabha polls. Although he won the elections the second time over, he was still a long way off from winning the hearts of his community as their political representative in Delhi.

By 1984, although Charanjit Singh was an influential member of the Lok Sabha, and part of the inner coterie of Delhi's political circle, it did not insulate him from the violence in the aftermath of Indira Gandhi's assassination—three of his Campa Cola bottling plants were wrecked by mobs, an act which Khushwant Singh implied was due to the involvement of a "rival manufacturer of soft drinks". Thereafter, it was a long haul for him, initially in securing licenses to replace damaged or destroyed machinery and later in overcoming the "technical objections" raised by the Customs Department. Charanjit Singh was routinely harassed by a hostile bureaucracy in whose mind, an affluent Sikh had "got away" easy. It was during this phase of vilification that he found acceptance amongst Delhi's Sikhs who interpreted every affront towards an eminent Sikh as an insult to the community. Finally, when he was denied a party nomination by the Rajiv-led Congress party and excluded from the cabal of the political elite, the Sikh community accepted him as their own.

Charanjit Singh was the last Sikh to be fielded by a political party until Dr Manmohan Singh who lost as a Congress nominee from South Delhi in 1999. It took another fifteen years before Jarnail Singh (who gained notoriety for throwing a shoe at ex-Home Minister, P Chidambaram) was nominated by the Aam Aadmi Party (AAP) from west Delhi in 2014, and lost the elections in the wake of a Modi wave in the country.

❀ ❀ ❀ ❀

Prior to 1984, political involvement amongst Delhi's Sikhs was restricted to Sikh shrines or gurudwaras. It gave them power and there was pelf to be had as the Delhi Sikh Gurudwara Management Committee or DSGMC managed ten gurudwaras, thirty-nine educational institutions including schools, colleges, and technical institutes, besides running three hospitals.

The control of Delhi's gurudwaras was first vested with the community by the British under an archaic Act of 1914, which was replaced in 1925 by a law which mandated the Shiromani

Gurdwara Parbandhak Committee (SGPC) in Amritsar to take charge of all the gurudwaras in the country and since then, Sikh shrines in the capital remained under its control for almost five decades till 1971.

When the Empire shifted its capital from Calcutta to Delhi and began the process of constructing New Delhi around the Raisina Hills, it illegally encroached on land belonging to Gurudwara Rakabganj, a shrine of great historical significance. The matter was settled amicably after the British withdrew their claim but resurfaced in 1960 when the Delhi administration wanted control over the plot of land. The Sikhs erupted in anger and the agitation catapulted Jathedar Santokh Singh as an important leader of the community in Delhi.

A decade later in 1971, it was the turn of a one-time Akali Dal Lok Sabha member from Sangrur, Bibi Nirlep Kaur who along with a group of miscreants attempted to wrest control of Delhi's gurudwaras, which resulted in violent clashes amongst Sikhs. The incident led to the enactment of the Delhi Sikh Gurudwara Management Act in 1971 with a specific intent to protect the shrines in the capital. Under the new law, members of the Delhi Sikh Gurudwara Management Committee were to be elected by Delhi's Sikhs and the Congress sensing an opportunity to gain control of the gurudwaras began its backroom parleys. However by the mid-1970s, the political situation in Delhi was inexorably linked to that of Punjab and the Akalis held complete sway over the DSGMC.

The first elections for the DSGMC was held in 1975 and won predictably by the Akalis. Five years later, at the end of its first tenure, when the polls were held in 1979, the Akali Dal had split and Punjab was reeling under militancy. Indira Gandhi recognised a renewed opportunity and influenced the Centre to issue an Ordinance that no longer made it mandatory for a person seeking election as DSGMC President to be a matriculate, a high school graduate or even a Giani (a Sikh who is well versed in the scriptures). This paved the way for Santokh Singh to become president—almost as a reward for having set up two crucial and secret meetings between Indira Gandhi and Jarnail Singh Bhindranwale. It may be recalled that after  Jathedar Santokh Singh's assassination in 1981, Delhi's gurudwara politics was pushed deeper into the Punjab cauldron.

Santokh Singh's pre-eminence in leveraging the Punjab issue for Indira Gandhi was evident in an incident mentioned by the noted forensic expert and one-time director of the All India Institute of Medical Sciences, Dr T D Dogra. In a blog posted in May 2011, he claimed that Indira Gandhi had appeared "visibly disturbed" when she came enquiring about the Jathedar's autopsy in the hospital. Although the  Prime Minister kept away from the funeral rights, she was well  represented by Rajiv Gandhi and two  Cabinet ministers, Zail Singh and Buta Singh. But what was significant was the attendance  of Jarnail Singh Bhindranwale, at the Bhog ceremony of the slain leader.

❖ ❖ ❖ ❖

After November 1984, Charanjit Singh was replaced in Delhi by Lalit Maken who was listed as one of the main perpetrators of the anti-Sikh riots in "Who Are the Guilty?" (see chapter Eight, The Citizens Collective).

The Congress meanwhile followed a bizarre policy of distributing tickets to "tainted" MPs—while Sajjan Kumar and Dharam Das Shastri, MPs from Outer Delhi and Karol Bagh were dropped from the list, H K L Bhagat and Jagdish Tytler were re-nominated from East Delhi and Delhi Sadar respectively. In retrospect, Charanjit Singh was the only Congress leader whose political career ended rather  prematurely,  just as his life  had in 1991. After 1984, an eleven-year freeze was imposed on the DSGMC elections and with that Delhi's Sikh politicians felt completely marginalised and distanced from the Congress party.

However there was one man who played the game according to rules set by the Congress party and beat them to it – a small-time leader called Balwinder Singh who had filed an affidavit in the Misra Commission in support of H K L Bhagat in 1986. The

Commission took note of it and after citing it along with other pro-Bhagat testimonials, it exonerated the MP of all charges. Three years later, in the run-up to the parliamentary polls in 1989, Bhagat was presented with a *saropa* (a scarf or a length of cloth; a mark of honour in the Sikh tradition) by Balwinder Singh which later held him in good stead. In the Delhi assembly elections held in 1993, he was nominated by the Congress party to contest from the prestigious Krishna Nagar seat but lost to BJP's Harsh Vardhan.

In comparison to Balwinder Singh's political career which was cut short abruptly, his son had a successful run with the Congress party in Delhi. In May 2014, shortly after the party's electoral debacle in the parliamentary elections, Arvinder Singh Lovely (previously a minister in Sheila Dikshit's government) became the first Sikh to be appointed as president of the Delhi Pradesh Congress Committee (DPCC). Given his father's engagement with leaders accused of complicity in the anti-Sikh pogrom, it came as no surprise when the state Congress unit under Lovely's leadership chose Jagdish Tytler and Sajjan Kumar to campaign for the assembly polls in February 2015. Later when the Congress high command appointed Ajay Maken as the chief of the campaign committee, Lovely took umbrage and refused to contest the elections. However, he remained at the helm of the party's state unit until the election verdict after which Ajay Maken took over as president of the DPCC.

Lovely's political trajectory raises a question that has been addressed several times over in this book, albeit in different contexts: why do people exhibit different behavioural patterns despite undergoing the same experience? Why did a man (who was barely sixteen in 1984) choose to align with leaders accused of instigating rioters while others either ploughed for justice or remained confined to politics within the DSGMC?

Before attempting to comprehend the above-mentioned conundrum, it would be worthwhile to examine the political choices made by Sikhs in Delhi and Punjab in the aftermath of the 1984 riots. In the first Lok Sabha elections held after

November 1984, the Congress polled 49.1 per cent votes nationally, while in Delhi it secured an overwhelming 68.7 per cent and won in all the 7 seats. The two significant factors for the Congress party's victory in the capital were firstly, the high voter turnout which at one point was even higher than the average national figure and second, religious polarisation precipitated by a high-pitched electoral campaign. Although there is no empirical data to determine how the Sikhs had voted in these elections—whether or not they cast their lot with non-Congress parties—but it probably does not require great political insight to infer that they did not vote for the Congress in overwhelming numbers.

The first clear indication of an anti-Congress sentiment amongst Sikh voters was discernible during the Punjab assembly elections in September 1985. Despite the tragic circumstances of the preceding year, compounded by the shrill call for a poll boycott by terrorist groups, and the assassination of Sant Harchand Singh Longowal, Punjab turned up in full strength and registered a high turn out at 68.2 per cent. The Akali Dal secured a clear majority by winning 73 of the 117 seats, with a vote share of 38 per cent. Although at 37.9 per cent, the Congress was just a whisker away in terms of the overall vote share, yet it managed only 32 seats. The BJP contested on its own after severing an eighteen-year-old alliance with the Akalis and in the process managed to win only 6 seats.

The miniscule difference in the vote share between the Akalis and Congress was because the former had chosen to contest in fewer seats and its victory was primariy because of the 44 per cent of votes that it had obtained in seats contested. In contrast, the Congress stood at 37.9 per cent—a difference of more than six per cent and sufficient to justify the difference of 41 seats in the final tally.

The reason for Akali Dal's brilliant performance in the 1985 polls was obviously predicated on the support it had from the state's Sikhs who accounted for 60.8 per cent, whereas the Hindus added up to 36.9 per cent of the population. Since it can be safely presumed that the Akali Dal virtually drew a blank with the Hindus, it was 75 per cent of the Sikh vote which propelled the Dal to the top.

However things were on the mend from the mid-1990s after the Congress-ruled Centre initiated two major steps: the DSGMC elections in 1995 and the Punjab polls a year later, in 1996. For the Sikhs of Delhi, the resumption of gurudwara elections meant the Centre's acquiescence of the community's fundamental right to manage its religious institutions.

The historic 1995 elections were however swept by Akali Dal's Paramjit Singh Sarna who became president of the DSGMC, but after the Akali Dal split up in Punjab in the same year, Sarna formed a local breakaway unit in the capital called the Akali Dal (Delhi) by aligning with the Congress and remained at the helm of affairs for more than a decade till January 2013. Although the Congress had regained control over the capital's gurudwaras unscrupulously, it had the community's support which by now had altered its anti-Congress stance. The noted psephologist Sanjay Kumar in his book, *Changing Electoral Politics in Delhi: From Caste to Class,* observed that it is 'one of the popular misconceptions,' that the BJP is 'the first choice of Sikh voters.' He argued that although this may have been true for the 1984 elections, the situation began altering from 1993 onwards—in the 1998 assembly elections, the Congress had the support of 49.5 per cent of Sikhs as against 37.4 per cent who sided with the BJP.

According to surveys conducted by the Centre for Studies in Developing Societies (CSDS), there was a significant rise in Sikh support for the Congress between the Lok Sabha polls in 2004 and the state assembly elections in 2008. From 32.3 per cent in 2004, it increased to 41.7 per cent in 2008 and rose dramatically in the 2009 parliamentary polls when the Congress registered an all-time high of 57.7 per cent vote share amongst the community.

It is worthwhile to note here that the period after 2004 coincided with two significant events, the first was the official release of the Nanavati Commission report and second, a public apology for 1984 from a Sikh who also happened to be the Prime

Minister of a Congress-led government at the Centre. Although in the 2013 assembly elections, the Congress party's vote share dipped to 23.3 per cent and to 9.7 per cent during the historic 2014 parliamentary elections, the figures were indicative of Sikhs' voting behaviour mirroring the national sentiment. This was further bolstered during the 2015 assembly polls when both the BJP and Congress were vanquished by a fledgeling Aam Aadmi Party.

❀ ❀ ❀ ❀

After the Sikhs in Delhi drifted away from the Congress party in 2010, the Akali Dal won the DSGMC elections in 2013 and elected Manjit Singh G K as its president. As the son of Jathedar Santokh Singh, the man had interesting legacy. Manjit Singh G K was only twenty-three when his father was gunned down in 1981 and after cutting his teeth in several political parties, he finally made Akali Dal his home base.

Sikh politicians in Delhi can be typecast into three main prototypes. The first include men like Manjit Singh G K and Paramjit Singh Sarna who are  part of the political elite and possess both economic and social clout. This group also includes new entrants like Manjinder Singh Sirsa who steam-rolled his way to the top on the basis of his fabulous wealth and was elected the secretary of DSGMC in 2013, despite the fact that neither he nor his family were in Delhi during the 1984 carnage. In fact, the family acquired its surname, "Sirsa" from a district in Haryana bordering Punjab which was their home till two decades ago. As a child growing up in the Eighties, Manjinder was witness to his father's great ability in cultivating friends amongst local Congress leaders; Bhoopinder Singh Hooda, the former chief minister of Haryana, was apparently a frequent visitor to their home.

The father-son duo shifted to Delhi in 1995 and after realising the futility of rallying around Sikh leaders within the Congress, they hitched their wagon to the Akali Dal. Manjinder Singh entered the lucrative real estate business and became particularly close to Bikram Singh Majithia, who is the brother-in-law of Punjab's Deputy Chief Minister Sukhbir Singh Badal and younger brother of Union Minister for Food Processing, Harsimrat Kaur Badal. Soon, the gamble paid off and Sirsa was nominated as president of the Youth Akali Dal in Delhi. He fought the Delhi assembly elections as an Akali Dal candidate, first in 2008 which he lost but regained ground by winning it five years later in 2013. His uncanny ability to manoeuvre through political minefields was first evident in 2007 when he was elected as municipal councillor from west Delhi's Rajouri Garden. But in 2012, when the seat was reserved for women candidates mandated by an electoral fiat, the Sirsa family fielded Manjinder's wife, Satwinder Kaur Sirsa as a proxy candidate. The Sirsa couple jointly owned assets worth seventy crores including four luxury cars in 2012, and by 2013 their wealth rose by almost 500 per cent from Rs 43.36 crores to 235.51 crores!

In February 2015, Sirsa was pitted against Jarnail Singh, a Sikh leader who represents the second prototype and owes his political career to the shameful incident of shoe-chucking at ex-Union Home Minister, P Chidambaram. It may be recalled (see chapter One, Doomsday Delhi) that far from being part of the elite circle, he belonged to an economically backward class whose political consciousness was shaped by the November 1984 pogrom. He along with Jagdeep Singh and (a different) Jarnail Singh, have introduced a new dimension to Delhi's Sikh politicians as people who have firsthand and traumatic linkages to the riots but chose to join the Aam Aadmi Party which despite all its shortcomings is neither based on religious identity like the Akali Dal nor ambivalent like the Congress party about delivering justice for the victims of 1984.

The former Congress state president, Arvinder Singh Lovely shores up the third corner of the triangle—son of a junior Congress worker, his relentless work amongst his community to repose trust in the Congress party catapulted him into the political limelight. In 2003, Lovely was accused by the then home minister of Gujarat (now President of the BJP), Amit Shah for his involvement in a sex scandal while he was camping in Ahmedabad with two ministers from Punjab. Initially, Lovely had threatened to file a defamation case against Shah but eventually agreed to an out-of-court settlement. At a time when other Sikh politicians were strategising to present the best case before the Nanavati Commission, Lovely was embroiled in a sleazy controversy. But it neither deterred him nor impacted his rise in the Congress party.

Traditionally, although Sikh politicians in Delhi were denied pivotal positions both by the Congress and the BJP, Lovely succeeded in wrangling a ministership from the ex-Chief Minister of Delhi, Sheila Dikshit. Yet as the events in 2015 amply demonstrated, his position in the Congress is tenuous and largely dependent on the decisions taken by his party's high command. For Delhi's Sikh leaders, it is a perennial choice between the devil and the deep sea—while the Congress adopted the theory of co-opting them to their advantage, the BJP opted for the *outsourcing* model and left the Sikhs at the mercy of the Akali Dal.

So far as the Aam Aadmi Party and Delhi's Sikhs are concerned, despite the internal squabbles and severe challenges of governance, there is no gainsaying the fact that it is perhaps the only political outfit which provided  ordinary Sikhs with a platform to look beyond their religious identities. For instance, although the two Jarnail Singhs and Jagdeep Singh contested from constituencies that have a significant presence from their community, they were not merely known as "Sikh leaders" in the way Asaduddin Owasi of the Majlis-e-Ittehadul Muslimeen or several like him, are for the Muslims. In more ways than one, the future of Delhi's Sikhs will depend on how far the AAP succeeds in treating the community with dignity that has been denied to them for over three decades.

# Epilogue

The crowd surged towards  plastic chairs to sit under the arc lights. Several jostled and craned their necks for a better view. No one was complaining nor distracted by the Jimmy Jibs swinging wildly to catch the ecstasy in the air. Hundreds had gathered atop the terrace of Delhi's underground Palika Parking in the iconic Connaught Place or Rajiv Gandhi Chowk for a TV show in February 2015. The excitement was not over those who sat on the open proscenium but about exit polls which predicted a clear majority for the fledgling Aam Aadmi Party (AAP) in Delhi elections.

Raising his voice above the din, the Bharatiya Janata Party leader  flailed his arms and accused the news channel of packing the audience with AAP supporters. They booed in response. When the leader protested, the show's anchor turned to the audience and asked who amongst them was a  BJP supporter? A few hands went up in an instant; but the ones  in support of AAP altered the skyline. It was so different a couple of months ago,  I thought watching the jubilation from the stage where I sat as a commentator.

Someone in the audience grabbed the mike and spoke in  a staccato manner about the "undelivered"  promises made by the Narendra Modi government; a few others took the cue and shouted in support of Arvind Kejriwal and his team. It wasn't long before a middle-aged Sikh in his Forties caught the anchor's eye. His anonymity was of little consequence; his identity sufficed. He was agitated and did not share the enthusiasm of the exit poll results. Moreover, no one was in the mood for a lament but when he persevered, the crowd fell silent.

'I just want to ask Kejriwal if Sikhs will get justice? Will he seriously pursue his promise of punishing the perpetrators of 1984?'

Therafter he spoke continuously about the countless tragedies borne by Sikhs, the horror stories witnessed by several families— directly or obliquely. Sikhs, he said had cried themselves hoarse seeking redressal.

Several in the audience were astounded. After all, the crowds were in a celebratory mood; no one wanted to revisit unpleasant episodes which seemed passé that evening. But the Sikh was relentless and goaded the people to take a position. Soon the audience joined in the chorus shouting, "Punish the guilty!"

But it was easier said than done.

❈ ❈ ❈ ❈

On 12 February 2015, forty-eight hours after the most humiliating electoral defeat of his career, the Narendra Modi-led Centre ordered the formation of a Special Investigation Team (SIT) to probe the 1984 anti-Sikh riots. (The SIT is mandated to submit the report within six months of its formation). Two months prior on 29 December 2014, a little before the Delhi assembly elections were notified and the Model Code of Conduct had come  into force, the government enhanced the compensation for Sikhs by Rs 5,00,000.

Strangely, the announcements failed to evoke any euphoria amongst Delhi's Sikhs. The community had witnessed the formation of the Nanavati Commission fifteen years ago and had its hopes dashed after subsequent governments failed to press for trials following the publication of the report. The only consolation had been  Dr Manmohan Singh's public admission of remorse and with that  it had been curtains so far as  any official action  was concerned.

But after the Congress party's rout  in the November 2013 assembly polls in Delhi, there was a raucous demand seeking justice for the victims of  1984 survivors yet again.  In retrospect, the AAP government in its first forty-nine-day stint may have accomplished little except earning the moniker of fugitives, but it  had recommended  the formation of an SIT to probe the anti-Sikh riots. When the tide turned against Narendra Modi in 2015, his government made a belated attempt to regain Sikh support and swiftly  acted on AAP's initiatives. For several cynics, this sounded like the oft-repeated cliché—the  path to justice is  slow and tedious; there are several  pitfalls to be  crossed etc—but there is a significant difference in the current political narrative of the capital—the presence of two rival political parties who are bitterly opposed to the Congress, probably the only party that has reasons to prevent prosecutions. If the other two players, BJP and AAP hamper the wheels of justice, it will  be  at their own political peril.

Whether they suffered grave  personal loses or escaped  due to divine providence, almost every Sikh  family  kept the  memories of 1984 alive  by passing it on to the next generation. Even after three decades of the horrendous episode, there is intense grieving for those who died on the streets with tyres around their necks or were  hunted  down and trapped to be  murdered. The eerie rants of  murderous mobs are evoked each time there is a passing reference, an accurate recollection of the hysteria every time the nation mourns the death of a prime minister.

Although a commentator is  generally  expected to be non partisan during a TV debate,  I was tempted to shout across to the Sikh man that unfortunately, there can never be  a closure for the dead of 1984 and the closest one can get is by hoping for fair justice, which has so far remained elusive. In the countless interviews I conducted during the  writing of  this book, I was invariably asked  to pass on  an appeal to the government in power: recognise the enormity of the crime and seek atonement by beginning a fair trial against the accused.

While I was writing the last few words of this book, Salil Tripathi's *The Colonel Who Would Not Repent: The Bangladesh War and its Unquiet Legacy* landed on my desk for a  review. A poem that he saw inscribed on the wall of Jalladkhana Memorial in Mirpur, Dhaka—a mass grave during the war, has a similar affirmation albeit in a different context:

*Saakkhi Banglar rokto bheja mati*
*Saakkhi akasher chondro tara*
*Bhuli Nai shohider kono smriti*
*Bhulbo na kichhui amra*

The blood-stained soil of Bengal is our witness
So is the sky and so are the moon and stars
We haven't forgotten the memories of martyrs
We will not forget anything

Sadly, the ones who died in Delhi and elsewhere were no martyrs. Moreover, they did not die fighting a battle that was theirs.

# Select Bibliography


Chapter One: Doomsday Delhi

1. *Changing Delhi Through Changing Eyes*, W H Morris Jones, cited by many authors including Gyanesh Kudaisya and Tan Tai Yong in *The Aftermath of Partition in South Asia*, Routledge, 2000, p. 198.
2. Misra Commission Report, submitted to the government in August 1986.

Chapter Two: The Making of a Conflict

1. "Punjab Crisis and Unity of India", Paul Brass, in *India's Democracy: An Analysis of Changing State-Society Relations*, Ed., Atul Kohli, Princeton University Press, 1988, pp. 169–213.
2. "Sikh Fundamentalism: Translating History into Theory", Harjot Oberoi, in *Fundamentalisms and the State: Remaking Polities, Economies, and Militance*, Eds., Martin E. Marty & R Scott Appleby, University of Chicago Press, pp. 256–286.
3. *Bhindranwale: Myth and Reality*, Chand Joshi, Vikas Publishing, p. 5.
4. *Punjab: The Knights of Falsehood*, K P S Gill, Har-Anand Publications, p. 82.
5. *India Since Independence*, Bipan Chandra, Mridula Mukherjee, Aditya Mukherjee, Viking, 1999, pp. 433–436.
6. *India After Gandhi*, Ramachandra Guha, HarperCollins, 2007, pp.463–465.

Chapter Three: The Horror! The Horror!

1. *Life and Words: Violence and The Descent Into The Ordinary*, Veena Das, pp. 184–193.

Chapter Four: The Symbols of Violence

1. *The Great Partition: The Making of India and Pakistan*, Yasmin Khan, Yale University, p. 135.
2. *Sexual Violence Against Jewish Women During the Holocaust*, Eds., Sonja M Hedgepeth and Rochelle G Saidel, Brandeis University Press. It was the first academic book on the topic. Subsequently, the book inspired Gloria Steinem to launch the Women Under Siege project. She also declared that a better understanding of sexual violence during the Holocaust might have prevented such violence in later instances of genocide.
3. "Voices from a Scarred City: The Delhi Carnage in Perspective", Rajni Kothari, special issue of the *Lokayan Bulletin,* pp. 11-17.
4. "The Anti-Sikh Riots of 1984 in Delhi: Politicians, Criminals, and the Discourse of Communalism", Virginia van Dyke in *Riots and Pogroms,* Ed. Paul R. Brass, Macmillan Press.

Chapter Five: The Daughters of 1984

1. *A Ritual Slowly Unravels In India*, Rama Lakshmi, *Washington Post* March 29, 2009, http://www.washingtonpost.com/wp-dyn/content/article/2009/03/28/AR2009032801901.html

Chapter Eight: The Citizens Collective

1. *Delhi Riots: Three Days in the Life of a Nation*, Nandita Haksar, Uma Chakravarti, Lancer International, pp. 594–625.
2. "Voices from a Scarred City: The Delhi Carnage in Perspective", Harsh Sethi, Special issue of the *Lokayan* Bulletin, pp. 59–73.

Chapter Nine: The Art of 1984

1. *Delhi Riots: Three Days in the Life of a Nation*, Nandita Haksar, Uma Chakravarti, Lancer International.
2. *The Other Side of Silence: Voices from the Partition of India*, Urvashi Butalia, Penguin, 1998.
3. *The Shadow Lines*, Amitav Ghosh, Ravi Dayal Publisher, 1988.
4. *The Historical Novels of Bhai Vir Singh: Narratives of Sikh Nationhood, Volume 2*, C Christine Fair, University of Chicago, Department of South Asian Languages and Civilizations, 2004.

# ABOUT THE AUTHOR

Nilanjan Mukhopadhyay dropped college and picked up journalism as a career in the early 1980s. A well known political commentator, he writes for *The Economic Times, The Asian Age, Deccan Chronicle, Outlook, Amar Ujala, ABP Live, Business Standard and Business World*. Till recently, he presented a weekly show called, "A Page From History", showcasing historical debates and other issues on Lok Sabha TV.

In 2013 he wrote the critically acclaimed best seller, *Narendra Modi: The Man, The Times*, which was published by Westland/TRANQUEBAR. His first book was *The Demolition: India At The Crossroads*, in 1994. Nilanjan Mukhopadhyay is also a playwright and one of his plays has been performed by a leading amateur theatre group. He lives on the edge of Delhi, bordering Uttar Pradesh.

# ABOUT THE BOOK

'I want *sukh* (peace)—Won't you give me *sukh*?'
asked a middle-aged Shanti who witnessed the death of her three sons, one of them an infant, and her husband in a house torched with kerosene by marauding mobs; Dr Swaranpreet heard the woman in silence. The sixty-five-year-old Sikh woman from a west Delhi slum claimed that the police had inserted a stick inside her… Dr Swaranpreet examined her… she had been cruelly violated; He spoke a single sentence but repeated it twice in chaste Punjabi: 'Please give me a turban… I want nothing else…' These are voices begging for deliverance in the aftermath of Indira Gandhi's assassination in October-November 1984 in which 2,733 Sikhs were killed, burnt and exterminated by lumpens in Delhi. Several hundreds were killed elsewhere in the country. Nilanjan Mukhopadhyay walks us through one of the most shameful episodes of sectarian violence in post-Independent India and highlights the cruel apathy of subsequent governments towards Sikhs who paid a price for what was clearly a State-sponsored riot. Poignant, raw and most importantly, macabre, the personal histories culled over two years by the author, reveal how even after three decades, a community continues to battle for justice in its own country.

www.ingramcontent.com/pod-product-compliance
Lightning Source LLC
LaVergne TN
LVHW011011200726
843509LV00011B/1051